Angelica's Box

Copyright © 2015 by James Gordon

James Gordon A.K.A. Greatest Poet Alive
http://www.iblowyourmind.net/

Angelica's Box

By

Greatest Poet Alive

FOREWORD

It's good to be back. I mean, writing an international award-winning novel of mystery takes a bit out of you. And I did write a book of poetry to accompany the novel, "The Warmest Winter (A James Gordon Mystery)." I had to plug it just in case you somehow don't have it. (Shrugs) But it's time to return to the genre I love, and the one I'm the best at. Poetry!!

I met a woman working on the set of Chicago Fire, and we hit it off. It wasn't a romantic type of clicking, but it was there. Well, at the end of filming, I discovered she was married. It's a good thing that I wasn't looking for it to be more. Sheesh. It got me to thinking about my interactions with women and how they varied. Inspired, I began writing poems, but then the poems went beyond the women and just…became. The poems went left and right of what my original premise was in writing this book. This is a poet's psychotic, sober break on paper. Well, maybe not that extreme, but you get the idea. There is a lot of love, romance, lust, rejection, ego (ha ha), and other stuff. So, enjoy!!

Wait, the title. You're wondering about the title, right? My acting pal Nate gave me the name of the book. I told him about my encounter and her name. He said, "Call your next book of poetry 'Angelica's Box.'" The box is my thoughts and feelings. And now you know where the name came from. Enjoy. Oh, yeah. I'm back from never having left. WOOO!!

The Arrogance Mantra

as opposed to the hand-me-down humility once worn that is now discarded and donated,
i wear my confidence like a well-made, fitted suit upon a constantly chiseling physique.
so...
this will not fit you.

Lies (I Tell Myself)

I don't think of you, miss you, desire you, care about you, or anything that is synonymous with having any sort of affection for you.
These are lies that I tell myself so the contents of my heart do not overwhelm us both.

Lunch

We had lunch.
I invited her
But she treated.
Food was delicious, but allow clarity.

Said she was hungry
Her hands were on top of my head
Her palms placed themselves upon my heart
Her well-manicured nails reached deep inside me and
grabbed my soul.

Excused herself to the restroom and returned
Kissed my forehead where her hands had been before
Palms returned to where they had been
Fingernails went deeper than they were previous.

Realized that she removed all the thoughts negative, doubt,
and anything banal
Cleared my heart of all feelings of fear and hate
Cleansed my spirit of all the inequities that clung to it
And I realized, we had lunch.

The Truth

believe i am spoiling you
admit it
you like it

Further into Extreme

red nails contrast skin dark
time has begun and will not end
locked away from world
save for us, no one can hear screams

Hands

hold my hands said she
coincidence those are what composed the bra she was
wearing
so
held her hands did i

What (Looking at You)

What, her query when she realizes I'm staring.

My answer...

I thought I saw the most beautiful woman ever

Then, I looked away from you then back

And realize that now I'm looking at the most beautiful woman ever.

A Thursday Night (Parts 1 and 2)

I was late

It wasn't intentional

Told her I was on the way

Said she was waiting

Stopped to get more money

Always like to have more than less

Adrenaline flooded veins

Sweat on my brow

Parked caring not about or obtaining a ticket

Walked into restaurant, smiling, well-dressed, and with roses

Pink ones

She wasn't there.

She had left

She was gone

Counter girl and fellow workers laughed

Flowers given to a woman passing me by

Pulled ticket off window that needs to be paid

Drank four beers and two shots of Jameson

My mother laughed

Said get with your kind

Damn

Sitting here

Tie still in Windsor knot

Suit jacket occupying stool next

Natty is the personality of my clothes

Sitting here

Single malt of Jameson in two doses

Beer mug's contents now a triplet

Sobriety's calls and texts are ignored

Sitting here

Barmaid questions scowl frowning

Answers are one word at best

The music elevates the melancholy

Sitting here

Indulgence of alcoholic avoidance over

Twenty-five is percentage the tip left.

Intentionally bump larger man on the way out.

Sitting here

Car should drive itself

Ask and answer that I'm good to drive

House of Pain rides with me home.

Face First

Back porch of a Chicago bungalow

Season is summer but resembling spring

A gentle kiss has multiplied and accumulated passion

Breeze exposes nothingness under sundress

Legs widen with carnal instinct

Thighs part without Moses provoking

Waters rise and glisten

Beneath their surface, the darkness invites

Eyes wide with anticipation; forgive the cliché

Mouth watering mimicking the ocean below

Tongue will prove amphibious

And into the depths to find buried treasure I go; face first

Life (Live It)

Life
Right here, Right now
Not yesterday
Not tomorrow
Smile, Laugh, Dance, Sing (off-key even)
Do that ish
Life

Joyful Noise

My heart makes a joyful noise when she comes around.

Inspiration

She

You

Inspire me

So I write

Poems

My Meal

consume

devour

gobble

imbibe

ingest

swill

and if any of you remains

finish

Halloween Costume

Your costume should be me.
Custom fitted to your idiosyncrasies
And never would I have to be taken off.

2 AM

2 am request
to kiss you again
so i know first was real
then kiss you again
to affix second to reality
and so forth

5 am grateful
to receive your good morning text
because i have to leave early
but you don't have to be anywhere
yet you want me to know

9 am smiling
you sent me a picture
your curves and you
making my Brooks Brothers blue dress shirt
fashionable
and i like it a lot

11:38 am excited
call you during an infrequent break
you are curious to know about my day
mischief becomes you
telling that it is warming and waiting
exactly the message needed in front of the camera

2:23 pm curious
you ask what i want for dinner
knowing my mindset, you say besides that
we both laugh
i say pizza; you say K (after all it is a lady thing)
then you say, your dessert is taken care of

6:16 pm wrapped
i do not tell you this
simply run to my car, race from the lot, make a stop, then to
you, home
grabbed a bottle of what you like, flowers that you feel
similar about
pull up as you come out to greet
on the porch, kiss you with every second that i missed you
caring not how you knew

6:33 pm aroused
devoured well-made pizza of chicken sausage, mushrooms,
and spinach.
wash down with Coke Zero, but mind and body eagerly
desire dessert
as Martin reruns play on the screen, eyes, intentions, and
lips meet

6:37 pm devouring
gymnastics with no medals at stake
edge of sofa your hands form an anchor upon
thighs face downward upon my shoulders
eyes see only the shadow of your flesh
it would seem my hunger exists still
dessert is well prepared

6:53 pm intertwined
same edge of sofa

different angles explored
legs form a V shape
fingernails plant themselves into willing pectorals
crack in the drapes, hoping someone sees
piston movements and rebel yells
standing in it takes on literal meaning

lift you from edge of sofa
palms plant passionately on coffee table
random reckless smacks upon your ass with growing
intensity
only because you like it
as you and i engage in this canine carnality, wonder when
Gina says, "You go, boy," is she referencing me

carpet burns do not affect or bother dark skin
your eyes take all of me, as if angel were gazing from the
above
knead breasts and twist nipples gently then more
movements are serpentine and instinctive
a smile crosses your face at our mutual satisfaction
believe i am on a cloud not the carpet

you are where you need to be
and then some
your breath soft and sweet exhales and inhales upon me
meticulous the way your tongues lathers every inch of
phallus and the melanin that colors it
fingers show their expertise leaving nothing without
attention

8:47 pm relaxed
drinking a tall glass of coconut Ciroc and pineapple juice,
named Ciroc Obama
the wet spot is unavoidable because it is everywhere

Martin and Gina believe they have won the lottery
this is our favorite episode
you ask what time i have to be on set tomorrow
smiling, i say, "i don't"
we doze off as Gina jumps on the lottery official's back

1:33 am awoke
The Wayans Brothers are on now
you snuggle close to me, somewhere 'tween sleep and
awake
i kiss you because
this episode is when Marlon roasts his family at a comedy
show
it isn't bad at all

2 am request
to kiss you again
so i know first was real
then kiss you again
to affix second to reality
and so forth

What Say You?

You're either going to embrace this love
Or you're going to run for lower ground wrapped in sudden
fear.
Here goes...

From this point forward, I want to be with you, with you
only.
Clarifying what I mean so that it is plain as unseasoned
chicken.
This is the point where I want days, nights, and spaces to be
inhabited by only you.
Honestly, it's like that for me; the only thing missing is...

I enjoy the movies greatly, whether going to the theater or
watching on Netflix.
Bit of a nerd, so I indulge in video games, comic books,
and walking with a Beagle.
Love to eat many things except pork, and I enjoy grilling
and baking.
Oh, I like going out and staying in equally and whatever the
mood calls for; tell you these things because I know you
want to know me outside of me. (Chuckles)

There are days, nights, and evenings that my physical
presence won't be near you, and I ask your understanding

and patience.

See, I'm not that guy, never want to be that guy that you cut your eyes at.

Never want to be that guy that when you mention my name around family or friends, they say that I'm lazy or good for nothing.

Never want to be that guy that you look back years, months, weeks, and days and believe our duration was a waste, so I go act, perform, write, and whatever I need to do for us to be great.

You're a beautiful woman, in so many facets beyond the obvious.

You have options, whether past or probable.

There are friends around you that keep a collection of men around them for various and separate purposes.

That's all well and good, but I'm all the man you need.

There's no one else save for God that you need, no other place besides these loving arms, and there is nothing more mentally stimulating, emotionally resuscitating, spiritually matching, and sexually pleasuring than what I have here for you.

So...

I have told you everything that was on my mind and heart.

This is me with ego off like a superhero's mask and heart in hands.

What say you?

Thrust and Repeat

Sheets are five days of rainfall.
Upper molars and incisors leave imprints in pillowcases.
Hands embed themselves becoming inner thighs making
natural the lift.
Pedicured toes curl, while ankles are a Master Lock around
my waist.
Thrust, thrust, thrust, thrust, thrust, and repeat.

Her

Her

Ehr

Reh

Reh

Rhe

Her

All about...

Yeah

Yeah

Too busy fighting the good fight and plenty of other ones.

Too busy living up to the responsibility of being Slash, father, brother, and son.

Too busy battling demons that though vanquished still haunt me.

Too busy being convinced that there must be some trick to it that someone would genuinely want me.

Yeah

Concerned with the survival and advancement of people with the same skin.

Concerned with the survival and advancement of the Mama's boy within.

Concerned with doing good deeds so that I can gain redemption for my sins.

Concerned with looking at my bio and adding more accolades, achievements, and wins.

Yeah

These are excuses meant to dissuade disappointment and anger.

Never wanted or want to place your peace of mind in danger.

On the contrary, man in me would always treat you genteel like the black baby they put in a manger.

But I leave you at night because sometimes when I look in the mirror, I see a stranger.

Only would lie next to you
So you won't be
Lonely in your nightmare
And we can both embrace
What dreams may come
Then we can wake and...
Yeah

You remind me of a woman I should've met long ago.
Then, I wouldn't be searching for you now.
Wouldn't be watching you from a distance.
Wouldn't have wasted so much time.
We would be growing.
Yeah

Carnal Conundrum

Caught in carnal conundrum
Grips of your vortex holds me enthralled
Reality splits into unequal parts
Sanity loses itself

Caught in carnal conundrum
Teeth sink into melanin
Query if the juice is indeed sweeter
Sanity has amnesia

Caught in carnal conundrum
Orgasms have a cipher rhythm
Bodies create noises based upon friction and sweat icing
Shuddering now triggers fault lines
Sanity exists no longer

Racial Divide

Ethnic differences

Stigmas too much to overcome.

Well of affection deep.

Racial barriers are oceans.

The daydream was pleasant.

And I got you again.

Another Man's Treasure

only a few men have walked side by side with you

met one of the fortunate upon a short journey this past
Tuesday.

he spoke with vivid candor about she who had hastened his
demise.

described her features 'til there was no doubt the
similarities were all you.

listened as if circumstances were life-threatening to his tale.

watched his face light up as his recollections told through
epic narratives

sweat decorated his brow, breath shortened, and moments
were needed to find lost composure.

at the end, he recanted early premise and stated that
downfall was of his own devices.

turned to me and said that if i ever met a woman like the goddess he described, make sure that the path i walk will always be with her by my side.

patted his shoulder, told him that i would, and he nodded his approval.

rose to leave, but this knowledge i possessed would surely devour my insides

so leaning in close, calling you by name, and with a shark's grin on my face, told him thank you, and, calling you by name again, will be well taken care of.

One Woman

One woman
One woman is the main woman
One woman is the main woman and only one
Unlike a quarterback, point guard, or pitcher, no backup or
substitution needed
Trying to add to this formula is an express lane to disaster

One woman
One woman who is the main woman plus another woman
Figure switching names, affection, and beds is artistry
Usually the blind at some point develop sight
Light is shone on chicanery, and plot is discovered and
exposed
Then, there are no women

Women (I Love)

Let me know if you see yourself

Women who
are intelligent
are smart alecks (my Ma is)
are maternal
are confident

Women who
wear glasses
wear yoga pants/leggings
wear business suits
wear what looks good on them

Women who dig
sports
comic books
poetry
dark-skinned men with bald heads who are a little cocky
(shrugs)

Women who like to
read

exercise
eat
drink

Women that
tell you the straight-up truth
express themselves without fear
are about their business
carry it day in and day out

Women who are
poets
comedians
authors
storytellers

Women with
natural hair
great weaves
wear wigs
low cut

Women that are
curvy
tall
short
slim (with a few curves)

Women that are
Women...
Women...
Women...
Yeah, man.

8 AM (The Wakeup)

red nails tap melody upon obelisk

breath control more adept than a long-winded rapper

eyes hold eyes in a cobra's trance

pausing only to say good morning

indeed, it is

During Church

Church was crowded as usual, even in the overflow section. The Spirit was in the air from the way people were smiling and exchanging pleasantries. The choir was in rare form, and the soloist was spectacularly brilliant; she always was. And as the Pastor dove into his sermon, it happened!!

The words of the long-time Pastor's mouth made no sense. Yes, they were in a manly tone, but not the man at the pulpit. As Pastor began to grow more enthused, she remembered how he talked to her, told her to let it go. And how she did, let go.

Raising her fingers to feel the spot of her chin where he had cupped it aggressively, she then touched the nipple that was now trying to show through her silk blouse, recalling how his mouth, how his lips, and how his teeth took hold of it; the air conditioning was working perfectly, but sweat now coated her brow.

Similarly, the moisture began to develop elsewhere; she tried to cross her legs to quell the flow. It was an act of futility because her mind kept flashing back to last night, this morning. He handled with her the perfect mix of strength and gentility, caressing her body while thrusting to touch the very core of her soul. It was only two hours before service that she had been in throes that tempted, teased, and tortured her at this moment.

Why was she thinking of this now when there was nothing she could do about it? Service still had another hour, at least, to go. But no longer could she take it; the floodgates were straining to hold that which refused to be held any longer. She realized she had but no recourse, so out of her seat she leapt, clutching her chest, and yelling Alleluia!!! Over and over again, she exulted, fanning herself as she exited the sanctuary, telling everyone that it had gotten to her. The parishioners clapped vigorously, yelling their approval for her enthusiasm for the sermon. As she descended the steps that led down to the main floor, she reached in her purse and retrieved her cell phone. The text message told the recipient that church was over, and she was on her way back.

His Robe (On You)

You wake up with his presence no longer there, unclothed from nocturnal, carnal endeavors; the t-shirt you reach for normally would suffice to keep your body warm, but now, more is necessary.

From the bed, you slide on slippers, and begin journey across the carpet...eyes catch sight of a shirt, long-sleeved, laid over a chair. You pick it up, hold it against you, shake your head negatively, and replace it from whence it came. Continuing your search, chill bumps beginning to discover your skin, vision scanning, catching a glimpse of fruition only a few feet away; you still rush to the treasure you have sought, found.

It is blue, his favorite color on him, third on you; you begin to place it on you, and as you have the right arm inserted, you halt. Placing garment down, you reach at shoulders of t-shirt you're wearing, jerking it off of you and tossing it...somewhere...dancing on your toes to generate facsimile warmth, hastily you slide right then left arms in, and close it around you, smiling as if you've found something that doesn't belong to you. It doesn't, but you do not care.

Beyond warm but exhilaratingly hot, the chills are now goose bumps; the garment cloaks you with his warmth, his scent awakens your nose's sense of smell. The concept of being this close to him brings about the rushing as you dance around the bedroom; the full-length mirror catches sight of you, your cheeks are now blushing.

Looking at yourself staring at you, you flash the garment open and closed, thus exposing yourself to yourself…liking what you see. One, two, three steps, you leap onto the bed; turning, centerfold like, you face the mirror, look at the one above. Fingers, your own, travel your body, finding familiar places hoping, no, knowing, the pleasure that you yourself can create.

But you are interrupted. The door unlocks and is opened; he enters, stops, stares, and with a deep breath and a gulp with little composure, he tells you that his robe looks good on you; your fingers beckon him, as your voice tells him, "I know…"

Within These Walls

tad more warm than cold outside

theft of things infinitely moving everything going on

within these walls

the television blares on, perhaps questions of paternity

there are no questions, just declarations, exclamations

within these walls

room temperature is accelerated to resemble desert's
humidity

thunderous waves rage, roar, run rampant throughout

and against the barriers

within these walls

within these walls

sound is not contained

the manly grunts, feminine moans, wild beastly growls

friction tempts the barrier of sound and brings about the
merger

of things soft and hard

the result not ending is all becomes drenched

before, during, and after have no separation

no difference can be determined

within these walls

fingers intertwine as toes curl

sensual synchronicity

thrusts given and retorted places,

then other places, and ignored places all touched, kissed,

kissed, and touched

oh my

perhaps on a Tuesday, there is no need for existence

outside of here

so I will stay inside here and her

within these walls

Days into Nights

we have abandoned the external world

nothing out there but confusion, darkness, and people

and we are not confused

shadows are what we will be to each other

you and I the only people needed

clothes are a trail leading from couch to shower

from shower to dining room to bedroom

but not the bed

far too confining

we pause only to let tongues tango

there's only space around us not between

nails fresh from manicure dig deeper darkening dark skin

upper molars nibble on shoulder blades

toes touch ear lobes

thrusts have villainous intent

your well is indeed deep

and my hardened phallic stage surges forward, downward
to touch it

somewhere there are moans, screams, sounds that make

no earthly sense

our foreplay began this morning at brunch, and we have
been

contemplating consummating these latent orgasms since

I saw you walk towards friends of yours to speak

touched myself underneath the table in public;

my resistance was too weak

all four eyes of mine watched your posterior accentuation

move back and forth, switch and a half, left to right

11:22 am this was, and 11:57 pm it is now,

and so this is how we turn days into nights.

My Plate

served steaming hot

the moisture saturates the contents of the meal

every single category for nutrients satisfied

vegetables

meats

fluids

fruit

cheating pastry with loads of sugar to finish off

meal

ravenous the hunger, so I delve in like a great white with
stranded swimmers in the water

manners unnecessary as I only use my hands to hold plate

but with lips and tongue, no knives, forks, or spoons is how
meal is ate

smacking precedes licking, actually lapping of all things in
front of me

remnants on chin, the goatee, my shirt, and upon the legs
and lap of my pants

plan on devouring all of that once I get the chance

you offer me seconds, and for them, I can hardly wait

to eat again everything you put in front of me, even though there was never any food on my plate.

The Realm of Sensuality

No. No! We won't speak of things too fantastical

No overuse of similes, hyperbole, or metaphors

So let us go back to reality

Let us stand, both of us naked in the kitchen, perhaps
cooking, more than likely not alternate 'tween cold of
refrigerator but too close to oven, hot. You turn both waters
on, letting the water fill the sink til it overflows, trying not
hit your head on the faucet, or your chin on the sink. Good
china put away last night because experimental we are on
this table, palms placed on table mat settings, thrusts
moving frenetically to the shows on cable; pause only to
turn you over, pull you to edge, using my hands as a plate,
and having you as an appetizer, entrée, and dessert in this
early brunch. Believe this time gluttony would be
forgivable, but will save some of meal for lunch.

Adjourn not to the bedroom but bathroom; heading directly
for the tub. Intimacy comes to the forefront, having
prepared bubble bath…and every inch of you I cleanse and
rub. Believe that now I contrast my Sagittarius horoscope
the way I go under the water; I submerge…more water on

the floor outside of the tub than inside as the parts private of ours continuously merge. Again, the waters turned on but from the shower overhead. Directly under its powerful flow, we sit this time instead, baptized, cleansed, satisfied, all at the same time.

Sitting at my desk aroused again as I type this rhyme.

Whew

Like most folk, we make it to the bedroom and lie comfortably, not trying anything for the moment but indulge in intimate conversation and sleep; comforting thoughts of love and love coats our words as they originate in our mentality. Would be an aberration for most, but we have just experienced our reality of sensuality...

60 Minutes Before Midnight

candles lit

lights turned off

blinds closed

locks checked and secured

returning to you

with anticipation, my lips moistened, moisten the
magnificent land that is your skin; clothing long discarded,
you are the beauty as God made you. angry hunger
overcomes restraint, devouring the chocolate kisses that are
your mountains' peaks, your hands fiercely gripping my
bald head as I nibble nipples serving as placating palate. the
soft moans touching your lips are the only words we speak.
at 120 minutes before, we indulged in intimate, intricate
foreplay, but now as midnight approaches, the nocturnal
brings out the further freak...

pause from mountains' slopes and peaks to exchange
breaths that are the first of many; leave your kisses to
nibble nape of your neck, where I know your spot lies. as
stated earlier, forgive redundancy, but play fore completed;

male protagonist in erotic tale enters soaking cavern with feral thrust, enthusiastically, and rest assured, I have plenty. seventh letter spot mythical to most but to reach it and your orgasm, tonight I'll experiment as much as need be; exhaust the entire night, or resulting in obelisk's giving pornographic tries. poet's plan is to place a smile on your face that will continue throughout the day, while the face below continually cries.

dark skin of mine, skin of yours become one color, one skin, and one person bisexual has a different meaning as close as we are. secret count in my head trying to figure out...60 thrusts 60 thrusts 60 thrusts 60 thrusts 60 thrusts; lost my count so have to begin again this time in the jackknife, you know, you on your left side, left leg straight, right leg curved towards your chest high, me in between that crevice literally smacking your backside viciously with the left hand, while right hand stretches forward to tilt your chin. cerebral cortex aligned with spine from continuous back shots is how the orgasm begins with no fear of indictment, no absence of malice, as I push manhood into womanhood, trying to murder you. mischievous machinations are for my onslaught to lead from one to multiples; you scream continuously. it is a contrast for you to scream loudly and guttural like a hell hound, while you are beautiful like an angel from Heaven. you gaze towards your alarm clock; the smaller hand has touched eleven.

Bad Dreams about You

Had a nightmare, woke up a pole in a pole dancing class.
At first, wanted to wake up but couldn't let opportunity
pass. Accentuations of a goddess higher, lower, all sliding
up and down on me. No other man on the planet eyes could
envision, let alone see this, save for me. Estrogen combined
with adrenaline, then the stretching and flexing of muscles
and limb. Nightmare now a dreamscape because solo man
among beautiful, scantily clad woman, I was him. Now I'm
back in my house, sipping coffee, writing sensual poetry,
shaking my head because I wasn't there, in the midst of a
beautiful goddess doing her thing at a pole dancing class...

You walked into a room with a black dress shirt of mine on
and heels, strutting as if it were your own version of Flash
Dance. No garments, bra, or panties at all on your beautiful
person. A chair sits in this distance. You walk, no,
elegantly and confidently stride, towards it. The chair faces
you as you place the right, then the left leg on either side of
it, straddling. Leaning forward, nipples showing even
through black shirt, you tease the chair's back. Gyrations
from your lower self now grace the seat of the chair. Slight
leaking drops onto it because by yourself, from yourself,
you have aroused yourself. Up and down, left then right,

you hump furiously now till you get right there. And I am
privy to all of this, for I am the chair...

Long day at work, case of the Mondays, so guess they do
exist. As you enter door of your condo, you kick heels off,
discard business attire, and head towards the kitchen. You
pour a shot of tequila, drink it with a gulp, and then pour
another. The second one you carry with to the bathroom.
Turning on the bath to the right temperature, you then add
bubbles. After a short while, you enter. Taking short sips of
your drink, you ease into the comfort of the waters and
further release the stress of the day. At a point, you are
relaxed but wish to be relaxed further.

With higher knowledge of yourself and how to please you,
your fingers move with adeptness that no man has or will
ever have. As the swifter your fingers move, legs, knees
meet under water, and moans escape into the echoes of the
bathroom. Water begins to splash to and fro. Moans are
shrieks of exultation in ecstasy from you. And you are all
you need, for now. Again, I watch with intense fascination
for I am the water surrounding you...

These are my bad dreams about you; bad meaning good,
for I can envision them, but bad being bad, for I have not
lived them.

After the Shower

just emerged from shower, water dripping, ebony urge to
write something in my rawest form; no glasses, no clothes,
no stress, admiring myself and developing muscles,
wishing her whisper danced in my ear, hands roamed my
physical after I came out of the shower...

deodorant, olive oil, and a gentle spray of cologne clothes
me, left hand wipes sweat from brow; it is tossed aside with
a condescending wave. Begin to accept boxers then khakis,
but she makes herself visible and does not allow that.

growing to maturity steadily is obelisk from her touch;
kisses on my neck as if she had plotted, planting them
meticulously, moving from right to left shoulder while
carving her name on me with her lips. Her whisper
whispers without whispering that I belong to her...

my apologies...hard to type when being fondled,
consonants where vowels should be, vowels replacing
consonants...descendant from Transylvania she must be,
biting, but gentle bites leave marks in this man's dark skin.
am trying no longer to type for she has taken me away from
poem after I left the shower.

Nightmare on the Red Line

We decided this morning what we would do; drove
separate cars, arrived at separate times, parked in
McDonald's parking lot just to the west of the station. She
had arrived ahead of me, purchasing one-day passes. As
soon as I went towards her, abruptly she walks away,
dropping one of the passes. Picking it up and resuming
standing, I catch a glimpse of the red bottom of black heels
clicking towards stairway; watched as her calves, thighs,
posterior gave life to black leggings; black flowing top was
covered by short, black leather jacket. It gets cold at night
in Chicago, even in the springtime.

Arriving on the platform, we stand several feet apart. My
eyes never leave her; every now and then, her gaze finds
me. She shakes her head, laughing, but once she looks me
up and down, like a widow spider appraising prey. We
board different cars. She is on the very last car on the south
end, I am two cars north of her. The doors close, and I see
her thru the cars; it isn't hard because save for us, no one is
on the train.

She knows I'm watching, and as the train departs the
station she moves one car from me. I move to the south of

my car; she moves to the north of hers; the steel, the air, but nothing else separates us. Her smiles sends scribe so deep into affection; as if reading my thoughts, she leaves the window, discarding jacket. With a feline's grace she walks the length of the car, stopping, switching her butt back and forth. Returning in my direction, she has unbuttoned top; comes to the window smiling and leans forward. Moisture grips my mouth, oxygen nowhere to be found, then she covers herself as if I had seen that which was to be unseen. Coming forward again, with her lips close but not touching window, she mouths, "Touch it. Now."

In an obeying trance I comply, without hesitation; button, then zipper freedom, like a slave crossing through underground railroad, appendage finds way out of boxers. Opening, pulsating, swelling, throbbing, trembling, it begs to be touched, comforted. Looking up from dilemma, I look towards her. She nods approval, gazing into this universe that is hers, second only to God. Thumb at tip, fingers meet soon, grip softly, then gripping again, 1,12,22,31 strokes...eyes close, open, close, catching glimpses of her, and no longer is she there!! Fingers move my chin to where she stands over me, same seductive smile, "Do you need help with that?" We are at the 87th Street stop.

"Get up!" Her command again is met with no resistance. She sits where I once was; I stand in spot where she once stood, pulling khakis down far enough to have access to, but not so I resemble immature man. Rips boxers down front, her lips curl in a smirk at my hardness pointing at her; she kisses the tip, licks the beginning recess that wishes to escape manicured left hand's fingers that find, feel, fondle oft neglected undercarriage. Manicured right hand's fingers grab, pull, and squeeze my backside; her glossed, soft, moist lips capture where my thumb and her kiss had been. Eyes move upward, meeting mine, quick wink from right eye, eyes return to task performing from tip to base, her mouth and throat travel without ever taking in a follicle; no follicle taken in as she inhales, exhales hardness...only obelisk touches tender tonsils...no follicles multitasking...pulling and squeezing of my buttocks, multitasking...kneading undercarriage with gentle aggression all while lips treat appendage like a lollipop, ice cream cone, or like the chocolate left on the spoon when her mother baked. Lips lustfully lick length like that; if not for pole extending from floor to ceiling of train, legs shake wishing to buckle, buttocks tighten, only top of her head visible and not her motions faster than speed of train until...the train now pulls into 71[st.]

My lungs let out a deep exhale.

She rises to stand but first licks bare, few remnants left on her lips and me, the rest is gone. Swiftly turning to face where she was once sitting, pulling leggings down just enough, beautiful, begging, bountiful buttocks daring me taking a measured step backwards, she gives a teasing rub of her posterior against me. Back to life am; I smack, lightly smack, as if I was administrator administrating corporal punishment. Smack, as if I had violent vendetta against her buttocks in succession with maniacal exuberance, smack, smack, smack, smack, smack, smack,

smack. Smack, smack...smack!! Over her shoulder, she smiles, nods; soggy, dripping is her cavern from earlier escapades, my entrance acknowledged only by her gasp and opening, closing of speaking walls. Her height shorter than mine, significance is, while left smacks continuously, determined, darting, daring thrusts have life of their own...thrusting trying to tear tears from vaginal's happiness in the form of orgasms multiplied; my right hand lifts her head towards Heaven so that she calls to the Father. The reverberations from the barbaric back shots reach her central nervous system, then same right hand circles her throat, squeezing ever so slightly. Her curses merge with exultations to continue all things of debauchery that I'm doing.

My name has changed several times, compliments and derogatory terms, confession for another time...I am trying to commit murder. This vaginal, my vaginal, is willing victim. Am I even a man anymore? Savagely I pull her hair, smack her bottom, relieve her of oxygen; her screams scream throughout length and width of train. Lost count of my strokes at 322, started count again at 24, started count again at 24; nails have left traces in the seat's skin. She falls forward, I stand, villain with villainous intent forming in my mind and written on my face, her breathing heavy, body strewn across seats, waters of hers spilling underneath as well.

63rd, 55th, 47th have passed with Sox Park approaching. Regaining composure, she looks from me to lower self so similar to serpent as it moves back and forth, waiting again to strike. Familiar smile reborn, "Take it all," she says. I move towards her; she feigns fighting me off for scant moments, pushing her violently on her right side while pinning left leg high on pole. Human V shape, her legs with wide width, positioning myself to enter forbidden taboo entrance at edge, slowly softly, steadily, stealthily entering…she trying to relax but fear and longing have her conflicted. "Nooooooooooooo!!!! Stop!!!!!!! Do it now!!!!!!! Come on!!!!!!!" Then a deep voice.

"Dude!! Dude!!!" I turn to look at this man standing a few feet from me, "I thought you wanted to get off at 55th. The next stop is Cermak."

Black Leggings

normally, a gentleman, so forgive if scribe crosses borders of the inappropriate.

finally, eyes have seen glory in every poem before, so this is just a continuation of it.

words, similes, metaphors, literary terms fail in their significance.

ask forgiveness cause I haven't thought about anyone or anything else since.

watch your movements of my poetics come to life, such elegance, such grace.

normally, a tad bit overwhelmingly egotistical and gregarious but humbled by your space.

words from your mouth flowed as if waters by the Savior parted.

your departure had me feeling adolescent again, pleasure fully broken hearted

so I had to pen this after the break of dawn

all because she came with a beautiful mind, a spirited heart, insurmountable beauty,

and black leggings on...

The Difference

Query

What is the difference between leggings and yoga pants?

No man really cares or wants to know.

All that is important is that the woman fills them out, and they come off easily.

Query answered.

The Call

ignore insertion of batteries into mechanical man, no matter
how strong the urge fingers can carpal tunnel from finding
fountain's fictional space though on many nights you
have...found it do not pour that wine, tequila, etc. in order
to make submission easier, don't

too many nights have your legs wrapped themselves around
only themselves back arched from thrusts self-inflicted, as
if there were such a thing; blankets form facsimile partner
on top of you, as you simulate bite marks in his skin, in the
covers rising, pushing, sucking, then biting on your own
breasts and their peaks, like they were being done so by the
mouth and teeth of a lover's

it makes no sense, none at all; no one will question your
virtue sometimes, instead of carrying the repression, you
must find release this time, use your fingers to dial to
someone worthy and will make it worth your while...no
lovemaking singular tonight, make the call...

don't dry yourself; let it flow

Tonight

a half hour til you are done, quickly 'round our abode do I
run making sure everything is picked up, put in its place,
clean will be doorman, butler, cook, bartender, and waiter;
next time by you I am seen, you arrive from hump day,
glad you got over it, my aim is to help you get the day
behind you, forget

after taking your coat, I ease your sensible heels off your
feet, let me apologize for lack of detail, when you crossed
threshold, a double shot of Don Julio with lime is how my
love I greet you, tell me that I am so sweet, no, my reply, I
only performed my intuition of bringing what your friends
wish for to fruition

seat you at a table, room lit my by candles, appetizer crab
cakes, entree filet mignon well done, broccoli, dirty rice,
the strawberry cheesecake is more than you wish to handle,
three more glasses of tequila and your wardrobe for the
day; you start to dismantle but it is not time yet; you tell me
in inebriated sensual whispers how drenching, soaked the
chasm is wet

lead you to shower, undressing every stitch tonight; so glad
these places we did switch, so glad we did places switch,
waters running full throttle, spraying our skin, steam shades
the scene within, this is where the poem ends but our
excursion tonight begins

Oral Reciprocity

Only inches away, yet hating the distance. My mind's kiss
upon your mental, you feign to resist. My obelisk is a
hardened criminal, but surpassing granite. Manicured
fingernails frolic, faking fellatio. Poet, as indicated by
pulsating veins, cannot stand it. Sly smile crosses beautiful,
visible even in pitch dark. Soprano sings commanding me
to do your bidding. Addressing me as if you have
ownership. No resistance even if I wanted to. No resistance
even if I wanted to. No resistance…your aggression now
literal. Cataclysmic is the volcano's explosion. No lava
ever reaches the surface. Lava never reaches the surface.
Oh my, how the lava never touches the earth's surface.

I recover rapidly. You can place slumber at recesses of
your mind. Fixation is oral, 90 degree angles formed by
your elbows and knees. Posterior's outer shell parted by
eager hands. In Olympic diver fashion, face first my entry
into waters. Instead of 548, 1096 more appropriate, 120
licks swiftly. Same amount slowly, 48 circles, 14 figure
8's, 60 brushes upon the protrusion, 24 touches upon the
basin's floor, 730 alternating clockwise and
counterclockwise swirls. And with your orgasm's timely
arrival, I drown, again. Now we can begin…

The Three of Us

He suppresses cockiness with a poker face. Difficult knowing he is where most won't ever go. He applies the oil to dark skinned body so he will resemble flawless ebony. Anxious energy flows thru body, grasping obelisk and awakening its growth spurt. At the edge of his bed, he waits.

They join him. Pleasure is the purpose they have come for. And it's both for him and themselves. Lena is tall, slender, and dark. Ariel is voluptuous, tan, and of similar height. They are dressed in black, his favorite. Sipping, sharing vodka from the same glass; intimately close as if the women had been lovers themselves. They are. They approach…

On his back they push him, left and right hands on his chest. Lips of hers engulf the tip of his hardness, while lips of hers devour its sides. The sounds are reminiscent of famished females lapping up remnants. His equilibrium spins, loses its balance, and he wonders where time went. They exchange places, until the syrupy snow becomes their lipstick. With the chocolate cone still made of granite, they remove remnants so obelisk is as it began. Now he begins his assault; Ariel is now on her back.

He enters her flowing, fruitful fountain. He then motions for Lena to come from making drinks. She places the drinks down and obeys his command. With his left hand he takes hold of her right hand. A mischievous smile takes over Ariel's face; Lena's lips merged with Ariel's, while Lena's chalice to his mouth. It is a triangle or human wheelbarrow formed when all lovers are in place.

The scene of debauchery is of proportions epic. Passionate and deep kisses 'tween the women intensify, while his thrusts of granite and geometric movements of his tongue are a pace frenetic; minutes pass minutes pass minutes pass but still, they have not slowed debate which has reached louder decibels, the moans and screams or the friction combined with the moisture created the point is irrelevant and mute. He seems to plunge deeper, deeper, and deeper still, with both of his erotic appendages his prey, both high and low, reciprocate in kind. The scent of this interlude is in the air; limbs begin to falter, yet are renewed. Nectar down his esophagus, intoxicating as if from Tree of Life, had been brewed one, two, three; loud, louder, and even louder the orgasms, then the screams come.

They collapse in a hedonistic heap man on top of woman, woman on top of woman, breathing heavily, words not spoken. Waters of Venus and Mars are the ocean they tread on, now waiting for mere moments to begin anew.

Interlude

Somewhere in the midst of writing this, something went awry, left, or not necessarily right. The passion inside of me had no channel to focus it, so a boiling over was highly probable. I lost it!!! There were encounters with people that had a bit more hostility than the situation would normally call for. Then, I enjoy a cold beer…okay, beers…and a shot of Jameson, but then I didn't want that as much. Don't get me wrong, a tall glass of Green Line Beer is irresistible. Still, I didn't drink with the frequency that had always been with me. Yet, there had to be some way to rid myself of all this chaotic energy that was growing and threatening to consume me. What, though?

And it came to me!! As I was driving home from a storytelling event, I realized that I was no longer riding home by myself. There was now someone sitting in the passenger seat. And it was unnerving because he looked exactly like me!! He was different. The aura radiated with more confidence that I ever had, even as G.P.A. He was leaner, with more muscle. His clothes were tailored to his physique, and it was obvious that he had an attitude. This attitude was unwavering, cocky, and I dare say, a bit mean. He spoke to me without words and told me to pull over. Once I did, he began to detail what direction this book and life would go. He chastised me for not being aggressive enough, ambitious enough, and not gambling for even higher stakes than I had been. Admittedly, I was taken aback. I'm G.P.A., you know, award-winning this, champion that, blah blah blah. Right? I'm the man but he told me I could be more, be better, but he asked me a question that I never knew could be asked of me.

"G.P.A., how badly do you want to be the best?"

"I want it more than anything else."

"Good. Then, let me take it from here."

"Alright."

I did not know what all of this "letting him take it from here" would entail. The fact that the person telling me to do so looked and sounded like me made it easy to follow. But I had to know something.

"Wait! What do I call you?"

"Pizzle. Just Pizzle." And he opened the car door, stepped out into traffic, and was gone like Kevin Spacey's character was at the end of "The Usual Suspects." It is worth noting that I never slowed the car down on Lake Shore Drive. Pizzle, huh? Alright, let's do it!!

Now the mystery that some of my friends have been consistently asking me about is revealed. I have to confess that I wasn't truly sure who Pizzle was to me when I met him, these months I have gotten to know him, but as of right now, I get it. Also, he said that his name must be said with a whisper. So it's (soft whisper) Pizzle...Now, back to the masterpiece of "Angelica's Box."

Angelica's Box (Pizzle's Turn)

This Love (On You)

when i put this love on you,
to whomever you pray to,
you will give thanks.
in proving your gratitude,
everything you will do so that
i hasten to and remain in your life.
and nothing will you do
to make me ready to depart.
in this,
all memories of hurt and loneliness
will exist as if they never did.
when i put this love on you.
Pizzle

Text Back (Part One)

You would probably get a text back,

If Pizzle felt like texting you back.

If Pizzle didn't think your posts came across as angry, bipolar, desperate, and mean.

If Pizzle didn't wonder why we exchanged numbers in the first place.

If Pizzle wasn't busy.

Eff Humility (A Haiku)

being humble gets

you praised by people waiting

to go right by you

Love Loves Me

something about you

makes me foolishly believe

love may just love me

Pizzle's Disinterest

Had to leave her presence

No longer was my heart inspired

To beat furiously

Pizzle is Excellence

Even if I slipped into mediocrity somehow, it would be excellent.

Wrong Choice (She Made)

chose the pretty boy

became an epic failure

made you feel ugly

Pizzle's Mission

obsessed with being something greater than myself

Us...

Reciprocity

Only want your attention to keep it

Then I can give you similar

Reciprocity

Pizzle's Optimism

there is a war on the people of melanin

the greatest city i call my own is saturated with violence

and yet, as i take another breath and wipe tears away,

there is reason to smile

still

Pizzle's Thirst

lack of hydration

no bottles, cups, or faucets

recourse is inevitable

you are holding libation suitable

yet, would rather have me

thirsty.

Pizzle's Mocking

nothing wrong with wanting what you want

not at all

you were in the midst of being cuffed

dodged, ducked, and weaved (not a hair reference)
courtship

wasn't going to settle

that makes sense, sure

hopefully, that choice will be the embraces, kisses, and
warmth that you need

it gets quite cold

The Fascination with C's

colder climate

cuddle constantly

comforting cocoa

claiming covers

come closer

Case of C's

Fools Rush In

fools rush in

actions impetuous

words reckless

hearts racing

feet moving faster than rationale

fools rush in

Dress You Up

After I have cleansed you thoroughly
With a towel will dry you off
Then with my hands moisturize your skin
Finally, will apply the perfume that will be my kisses to all
the places that make up your body
But I'm getting ahead of myself
Going to dress you up.

When he sees you in your new clothes, nightmares of his
loss will haunt
Foes in the guise of friends will breathe envy
No longer ahead of myself
This is what happens
When you are dressed properly
Dress you up.

A bit presumptuous am I
Bought your size in the Giuseppe's you wanted
Hand upon each calf in turn, as I slide them on each foot
But I'm getting ahead of myself
Going to dress you up.

Dress you up
Only to undress
So I can then dress you in ferocious and unrelenting
passion
But wait, I'm getting ahead of myself
Going to dress you up.

Going to turn the water on a comfortable warm
Pour the bubbles in so that they surround and engulf you
Tell you to lean back so that I can cleanse you
Wait, I'm getting ahead of myself
Going to dress you up.

Going to put you in this white Brooks Brothers dress shirt
and button it until your cleavage begins
Wait, I'm getting ahead of myself
But I'm going to dress you up.

I want to take my silk tie off and tie a Windsor knot around
your neck.
Wait, ahead of myself
Have to let you rest after a long week
But I'm going to dress you up.

Pizzle's Promises

under a full sun and beaming moon
nightmares of loving you
knowing full well that you made promises to another
unbeknownst to you, similar promises my heart made

promised that another would never inhabit my intimate
thoughts
promised that this bed would only hold your body and scent
promised that my heart would only hold your signature for
ownership
promised that....

in the light of darkness
whispering loudly these vows
knowing full well that you made promises to another
i made promises to you

Text Back (Part Two)

You probably would have received a text back

If G.P.A. was not busy electrifying a crowd

If G.P.A. was not recording his soothing baritone

If G.P.A. was not utilizing his role as a background celebrity

If G.P.A. was not in the middle of furthering his muscle mass

G.P.A. was busy

So

i am not from Mars; sure women are not from Venus
aware that both are planets and gods from Greek
Mythology
besides that, nothing to do with us
so...

complexity of interacting the way we are supposed to is
unnecessary
we were created for, destined for, and meant for each other
no more gymnastics, intense interrogations, or hoops to
jump through
one plus one equals two working as one; it is that simple
so...

never seen perfection since receiving 100 on a test score
in our imperfections, we can find each other's similarities
it is as we were created, so like rubbish, let's throw
unrealistic expectations in the trash, and love
so...

Pizzle's Plan

would just be easier
if we loved on each other,
shared everything,
and had sex like tomorrow was the Apocalypse

The Truth

Do not lie for my benefit

Tell them I mean as much to you as nobody means to
somebody.

After all, that is the truth.

Isn't it?

Different (Thought You Were)

thought you were different
quoted scriptures so adamantly and eloquently that i looked
up each one
asked if there were other men beside me, and believed like
a good Christian when you said there were none
and you said that when you pulled a disappearing act that
you were speaking with Him, and then we were done
if you truly loved me, you would have given some notice
you were leaving, right?

thought you were different
perhaps the male protagonist is being petty
thought my impression was enough that your heart would
never forget me
seems in a blink of an eye you did so successfully
then i remembered that Lucifer speaks melodiously and is
quite pretty
if you truly loved me, you would think more about me than
yourself and not hurt me, right?

Pizzle's Query

Sips Gatorade
Composes heart's words
Removes glasses
Smiles and looks into your pools of depth
One of two things are going to occur when I'm done
You're either going to embrace this love
Or you're going to run for lower ground wrapped in sudden
fear

Here goes...
From this point forward, I want to be with you, with you
only.
Clarifying what I mean so that it is plain as unseasoned
chicken
This is the point where I want days, nights, and spaces to be
inhabited by only you.
Honestly, it's like that for me now; the only thing missing
is...

I enjoy the movies greatly, whether going to the theater or
watching on Netflix.
Bit of a nerd, so I indulge in video games, comic books,
and walking with a Beagle.
Love to eat many things except pork, and I enjoy grilling
and baking.
Oh, I like going out and staying in equally and whatever the
mood calls for; tell you these things because I know you

want to know me outside of me. (Chuckles)

There are days, nights, and evenings that my physical presence won't be near you, and I ask your understanding and patience.

See, I'm not that guy, never want to be that guy that you cut your eyes at.

Never want to be that guy that when you mention my name around family or friends, they say that I'm lazy or good for nothing.

Never want to be that guy that you look back years, months, weeks, and days and believe our duration was a waste, so I go act, perform, write, and whatever I need to do for us to be great.

You're a beautiful woman, in so many facets beyond the obvious.

You have options, whether past or probable.

There are friends around you that keep a collection of men around them for various and separate purposes.

That's all well and good, but I'm all the man you need. There's no one else save for God that you need, no other place besides these loving arms, and there is nothing more mentally stimulating, emotionally resuscitating, spiritually matching, and sexually pleasuring than what I have here for you.

So...

I have told you everything that was on my mind and heart. This is me with ego off like a superhero's mask and heart in hands.

What say you?

The Pocket Square (Her Black Panties)

quizzical expression birthed upon countenance
eyes searching as if answer were in plain view
curiosity's hands push human ones to grasp
fabric was made with great care
scent as if they had arrived from the place they were
created
smirk now lives upon my face; cognizance creates clarity.
remembering from where and who this black thong came
from

asked where i kept them and replied with a chuckle
in my back left pocket of everything i wear
i keep them there, close
at various times today, i will remove and inhale them
just in case, i can...

Woman in a Yellow Dress

yellow fabric illuminated by melanin
green with envy of garment so close to her skin
waking and walking night is she, for she is not in close
distance
pray that in a nonexistent whisper she call out my name,
and to her side i go without resistance.

Pizzle's Invitation

dinner and a movie is how it starts
lunch in Hyde Park is the continuance
breakfast overlooking downtown renews
let desserts be the moments in between
delusions of a poetic unsub on a humid Wednesday
care to join me?

Home (Where Pizzle Wants to Be)

there is no place like home
home is where the heart is
give my heart to you
so I'll have home to go to

Narcissistic (The Ego of Pizzle)

I blinked

Found myself in a moment of introspection

Not surprised by the developments that played out like a 3d movie

Listen

Turned my hands palms up, and it was day

Turned them the opposite, then night arrived

Shaved my head bald so that no land would be barren

The sweat from my brow, though small, provided rain; farmers would never worry about droughts.

Had dialogue with Stephen King, Alfred Hitchcock, Clive Barker, and Rod Serling about bad dreams I had, thus spawning books, TV shows, and movies that will define horror and suspense.

Conversely, the fantasies floating through my mind are depicted in the Songs of Solomon and what every lover aspires to but never reaches.

When I run, my feet leave Barry Allen, Eobard Thawne, and Pietro Romonov in the dust.

Superman and every creature with wings follow my flight plan when I take to the air.

And all the inhabitants of the sea, Aquaman, Namor, and Neptune imitate my strokes; my name is Leviathan.

Women want to be with me, whether single or taken.

A glance from me causes their hearts to stop then rage, threatening to leap from their breasts.

My voice is such a hypnotic tango; when it caresses their ears, the effect is of Lorelei or Pied Piper.

And if I place a finger upon their flesh, willingly they give themselves for a day plus eternity.

Such a heartthrob am I?

Every moment in the past, present, and future, my presence has influence.

Stepped in front of the bullets that would've slain Kennedy, King, Lincoln, and X, eradicated the African Slave trade, prevented the Holocaust, stopped the bombing of both Hiroshima and Pearl Harbor, made everyone color blind, kept the towers from being hit on 9/11, rendered guns useless at Columbine, Colorado, Virginia Tech, and Northern Illinois, and paid teachers what professional athletes make.

But before all of that, I tapped the Almighty on the shoulder Saturday night to let him know that I'll take care of Sunday.

Smiled at this reflection.

Then I blinked

And realized that not only was my ego tripping, but it's that Pizzle is narcissistic.

Simple

I'd like to pick you up in my new car.
Open the door, admire longingly at you, and compliment
your new outfit and shoes.
There's a new thriller that just came out we can see.
And further north, let's try this new restaurant.
In the beginning, middle, and end of the night, let's kiss as
if we had never before.
Yeah, brand new like.
That way, this way, it never gets old.

Now Come Here

Darling, Sweetheart, Baby, Honey, Love
Have a seat.
No, leave your phone where it is; this won't take long.
But I need for you to hear me and listen.
I know and appreciate the woman you are.
Capable, brilliant, talented, multifaceted, and of course,
breathtakingly stunning.
Believe me, I know that I'm winning with you.
But more often than not, even with all of those tremendous
qualities, I need you to get behind.
Don't look like that.
What I mean is that I'm a man, your man, so...
I got this.
I got you.
That's all.
Appreciate you listening.
Now come here...

Orgasms from Scratch (Intro)

unlike cornbread muffins

there isn't Jiffy Mix for Orgasms

Pizzle makes 'em from scratch

(chuckles and shrugs)

Orgasms from Scratch (The Text Message)

Text message from Her: After a long day, orgasms from scratch would hit the spot

Pizzle: That's the idea

Her: Mmmm

Feed Me

Thursday through tempting teasing once I was at your feet,
and appetizers are your toes
reference Kottyn Campbell's book about me when I say
forget peaches, rather devour mangoes
such an angel so you are so aspire to cunnilingus create
cherubim's catastrophic cataclysms
immerse intimately inside so deep that your belief might be
that I'm one of your chasm's organisms

inhale the fragrance permeating the atmosphere til it
becomes instinctive to do so
when asked what clings to this melanin, respond that the
perfume is called "her" so that everyone knows
enlightened and satisfied by the dining experience that
walking around in a gluttonous haze
so when my mouth says that hungry am I still, feed me, and
do not be amazed.

Metaphors of Permanence

I am the monster under the bed.
I am the Boogeyman in the closet, but when you come with
your friends to verify my existence, I am not there.
When you come to retrieve your jacket or coat, I am the
one handing it to you, fangs glistening in the moonlight
with saliva dripping from my mouth, for I am ravenous. I
am Jason Voorhees, Michael Meyers, Freddy Krueger,
Pinhead, and Pennywise, and no matter how many times
you wish to kill or vanquish me, another movie or book is
made for me to live again.

I am Lex Luthor, the Joker, Professor Zoom, Simon Bar
Sinister, and Riff Raff, and the heroes that battle, for this
illustrates the perpetual struggle of good versus evil. I am
the proverbial fly in the ointment that shows up at the
picnic, and no matter how much you swing and swat at me,
I do not leave but tap dance in the potato salad, perform
backstrokes in cole slaw, and swing back and forth on your
fork as you are getting ready to place it in your mouth.

And these are the metaphors of permanence of what I truly
am.

I am the anger and hatred of Beelzebub for being cast out
of Heaven, and I am the disappointment and resignation of
the Almighty Himself knowing that when He created
Lucifer, He would have no recourse.

I am the bully, the bullied, and the bullied that finally stood up to the bully. I am dark skin, for no matter how many times it has been chained, whipped, or cursed, it and the people who have it, remain.

And these are the metaphors of permanence to show what I truly am.

I am an addict, but there are no pipes, blunts, bottles, or needles. There is simply me going to open mics, using assumed names, taking the three, five, or how many minutes given to me, and performing like I'm the feature.

There is me using social network to share a poem so there is room for the next poem and the next in my head. I am the invitation in the mail sent to me, and it is an invite that I am surprised that I received. At this gala, there is Wordsworth and Blake conversing in one corner, while Giovanni, Hughes, and Brooks exchange stories in another. I bow my head in reverence as Maya Angelou approaches, but she lifts my head by the chin and says, "Welcome home, my child."

No longer am I lost or wayward.
My life has a course and high purpose.
This skin is temporary and irrelevant, for I realize what I truly am. I am a poet.
And the metaphors of permanence are complete.

The Arrival

It is close to midnight as I'm writing this, which makes it a splendid time to speak to you myself. Do you realize the privilege that I am extending to you by stepping out of moments of my existence to come down to these lowly depths to speak with you? Of course, you cannot. So beyond your comprehension is the mere thought of me that your demise would surely be a blessing. There comes a moment in your life when it turns, when a grand epiphany occurs, and afterwards, you'll never be the same again. This is that moment. You have been wondering who I am, what I am, and when I was coming. I am Pizzle. But even though the very inkling of an inkling of my existence is magnanimous, you must pronounce my name with the slightest whisper. Why? To truly extend an explanation to you would crush the mental capacity of your bloodline for centuries to come. Simply put, my name must be spoken in a whisper as to pay homage to my greatness. It is only right. So it goes like this: (soft whisper) Pizzle. That's it. Now, I know you're enjoying this masterpiece of poetic genius by G.P.A. under my superior leadership that is "Angelica's Box." Yes, you can have some more Poetry from us. (insert sinister laugh)

Text Back (The Conclusion)

Soon as I wake up,
When they wrap for the day,
As soon as I get to a red light, stop sign, or pull over
because I'm driving,
Once Scooter and I return from our walk,
You will get a text back.

Carry It (Sometimes)

days when morning becomes morning, and night was a
casual observer
moments when the energy level may be low, but the grind
calls caring not
when you think you see or hear something that may raise
your eyebrows or temper
money stretches to cover everything it is supposed to, yet
stretches not much farther

don't need you to pick up half or ever more than that
just a little bit some time
99.8 percent of circumstances, I've got this
but sometimes, I need you to carry it.

Please (Don't Stand)

Police reference, and beautiful woman inspired...

Please don't stand so close to me.
I can hear your words just fine from that distance.
But the more you speak, the more I have to listen.
As you know, etiquette dictates that you look into a
person's eyes when that individual is speaking.
Now, every syllable you utter takes shape and forces me to
listen intently.

Please don't stand so close to me.
Glasses intensify vision.
Your hair movements when your head tilts one way or the
other
How your jeans fit close to your waist, grab a hold of legs,
and become relevant because you are wearing them.
That blouse's skin color is now second fiddle to your own,
but I see this scenario because your accentuations give the
fabric life.
And I want coexistence.

Please don't stand so close to me.
Listen, you are a beautiful woman.
Your conversation has a combination of articulation, levity,
and substance.
It is a blessing to be in your presence, at this close
proximity.

But when we leave, it will not be together.
So please...

City under Siege

Boondocks episode come to life

Streets with speeding cameras' lights turn red

Packages of promise torn up and dropped without care

Invisible lines of segregation are tangible

There is no rampant violence

Real estate value lowered to weed out undesirables and raise them again

Police are assassins in the plot under the guise of serving and protecting

From the inside of City Hall, my city is under siege.

Pizzle's Truth

Pizzle is not white.

Pizzle's skin is not light.

There was no silver spoon or trust fund that was attached to his birth.

The only popularity Pizzle's name garners is to be rooted against.

No opportunity to perform, feature, or interview has ever been offered to Pizzle.

Hollywood and society say that Pizzle's features are not attractive or camera worthy.

No group or clique is Pizzle's support system.

This stomach is not composed of a six-pack.

No manager guiding Pizzle's way

No promoter promoting Pizzle.

No publisher does the work for Pizzle

There are some facts here.

Here's how I see it

To Hell with white privilege and the racist doctrine that accompanies it.

Dark skin is from where all other shades are derived from and forms my armor

The spoons were always clean in my home and everything that I have I have earned.

I thoroughly enjoy being the bad guy, unsub, or villain.

Relentless aggression and being a tad overbearing has gotten me on stages, blogs, and such, and the people that listened, thanked me for it.

For all the negative stigmas thrown at me, every glance I take at myself, I get more attractive. And women see it and dig me.

I made my own team so I don't have to answer or be accountable to anyone but myself. And it's been working quite swell.

When I drank often, I could go get a six-pack. Otherwise, my stomach is not a bulging belly, and clothes look utterly perfect on me.

I got it.

I got it.

I got it.

The truth is I am the greatest embodiment of multiple talents that this age has seen, and I am evolving.

(Soft whisper) Pizzle

The Vow (What Pizzle Will Say)

Until God placed you in the sidewalk that is my life, I was lost, and that's me being honest.

So if I were in a room with a thousand women, so into you that I wouldn't notice them, as if your mind, spirit, and heart were homes inside a community that was Amish.

We both make mistakes because it's part of our human frailty and the way God created us, so in our imperfections let's strive towards perfection and never disparage, ridicule, or admonish.

I'm going to place this ring on your finger, walk down the aisle, jumped the broom, and get hitched, so long as no moment in any day do neither one of us feel like we are in bondage.

With my right hand to the Almighty and left hand on your heart, will love you, honor you, provide for and protect you, be faithful to you, learn from and educate you, this I swear and promise.

Epilogue

You have probably read this and thought, "This man is crazy." Good!! We wanted to give you a different experience when it came to reading a memoir in the guise of a poetry book. There is no one central train of thought that anyone follows, at least, not anyone who constantly swims in greatness like we do. If you have questions or feedback, please email us at gpa@iblowyourmind.net. This book was a series of rants and well thought out words, similar to our first book, "The Confessional Heart of a Man." There is no table of contents or one focus. We just gave you our feelings and thoughts on various things we encounter. Thank you for purchasing and reading.

We'd like to dedicate this book to our family members who stuck by us, gave unwavering support, and never judged us for being different. Thank you to all of the readers that support us without fail, no matter the endeavor each of us undertook. For all the individuals not mentioned above, meaning with favor, you backed the wrong team. Dummies!! And we're out!!!

My name is James Gordon. I have been kidnapped and I'm being held against my will. In no way would I have been a part of such a maniacal manifesto as the one you just finished reading. I write children's books. Please help me!!! Please! Help! Meeeeee!!!

www.ingramcontent.com/pod-product-compliance
Lightning Source LLC
Chambersburg PA
CBHW071201280526
45787CB00002B/558

Disclaimer Notice

Please note the information contained within this document is for educational and entertainment purposes only. Every attempt has been made to provide accurate, up to date and reliable complete information. No warranties of any kind are expressed or implied. Reader acknowledge that the author is not engaging in the rendering of legal, financial or professional advice.

By reading this document, the reader agrees that under no circumstances are we responsible for any losses, direct or indirect, which are incurred as a result of the use of information contained within this document, including, but not limited to, -- errors, omissions, or inaccuracies.

Table of Contents

Essential Oils for Relaxation

Guide to Perfect Relaxation and Stress Relief with Essential Oils

Introduction

I want to thank you for purchasing this Book, "Essential Oils for Relaxation"

Nature provides us with a bounty of natural ingredients that serve the dual purpose of healing and beautifying. I am sure that you have enjoyed a rejuvenating day at the spa and wondered what, exactly, is causing you to feel so relaxed.

Well, the answer lies in "Essential oils" and these oils will be present in almost every product that a spa would use on you. These oils are all natural and extracted directly from the source. The sources of these oils vary and right from trees to shrubs to flowers, several types of plants help in providing us with natural ingredients, which can help in healing our minds and bodies.

In this eBook, we look at the meaning of essential oils and look at how they are beneficial to mankind. We will also read up on the usefulness of these oils, in terms of providing relaxation.

As a bonus, the book will also carry out a few recipes, for oils, creams and other products that you can try out at home and reel in the true benefits of essential oils.

Let us begin.

Chapter 1:

What are Essential Oils?

In this first chapter, I ask and answer a few vital questions on the subject matter, so as to give you a glimpse of the magnificent world of essential oils.

What Are Essential Oils?

Essential oils are cold pressed oils that are extracted from the seeds, bark, leaves, roots and flowers of plants and trees. They trace their roots back to ancient Egypt, where people used essential oils as a means to gain therapy through aromas or aromatherapy. Ancient Mesopotamians used pots and other utensils to extract these oils and used them for their beautifying and healing benefits.

The trend then travelled across the world with the Greek, Chinese and Indians using it in their traditional medicines. The word "aromatherapy" was coined in 1937 by a French chemist and perfumer known as Rene Maurice Gattefosse, who is said to have healed his burnt hand with the use of lavender essential oil.

What Are Its Uses?

Essential oils are used for many purposes including beauty and medicine. When it comes to beauty, these oils are used in a lot of commercial and handmade products including beauty creams, soaps, lotions etc. they are also used in hair care products such as oils, shampoos, conditioners etc.

When it comes to its medicinal applications, these oils are used as an alternate method of healing and best used as supplements. They are known to help in reducing several types of illnesses that can be skin, hair or internal in nature. They are also used to treat brain disorders.

These oils are also quite popular as insect repellents and are known to effectively drive away mice, ticks, mosquitoes, etc.

How Are They Prepared?

Essential oils are prepared by many methods and each one has its own pros and cons. Some of the methods used to extract these oils include distillation, cold press, boiling, sponge extraction etc.

The most preferred way is to use a distiller, as it produces the purest form of essential oils. Several industries use this very form and you can also do this at home using a distiller. Another convenient way to extract oils is to use the boiling and distilling method, where the raw materials are boiled and strained and the oil is collected.

Where Can I Buy It?

Essential oils are easily gainable these days, owing to the growth in their popularity as effective beauty treatments. You can buy them from a drug store that also sells beauty products. There are also essential oil specialty stores that sell them.

You can also buy them from online stores and sites such as Amazon and eBay, where you can find a lot of sellers who deal with in these types of oils. But these oils can be a bit on the expensive side owing to the small output that the raw materials produce and so it will take a lot for the sellers to break into a profit.

Can I Make It Myself?

Yes. It is easy to make these oils at home, given that you have all the right equipment and all the best raw materials. You can buy yourself a distiller from one of the hardware stores or from online sites or you can easily build yourself one.

You can also adopt the carrier oil or boiling method, which will also help in yielding a near pure batch of essential oils.

Are They Really Useful?

Yes. Several studies have been conducted on the uses of these essential oils and it has been found that these have extreme medicinal and healing powers. In fact, many of the chemicals that are produced to fight certain skin conditions are created to mimic the functioning of these oils. As they are nothing but artificial clones of these oils many people prefer to use the real deal, as opposed to harsh chemicals, that can have side effects on human skin.

Do Essential Oils Have Side Effects?

No. since these are extracted from natural ingredients, they have little to no side effects. They might also not react with other chemicals that might be present in the body such as medicines and can be safely administered on people who are on medications. They are also safe to be administered on sensitive skin, which might not be suited to the use of commercial, chemical laden products.

Warning - Please only use Certified Pure Therapeutic Grade (CPTG) essential oils on your skin. These are certified as pure oils and do not contain any of the chemicals or fillers that cheaper or non-certified oils may contain.

Is It Safe For Everyone?

Yes and no. These essential oils are safe to be used on babies, toddlers, teens, adults and the elderly. They are safe for topical application and can be applied directly to skin, hair etc. However, it is advisable that you do not ingest essential oils unless there are specific instructions for you to do so. There is little evidence to show that ingestion of essential oils is not harmful and, as such, it should be avoided. It is also important for pregnant women not to do this, as they have been known to cause nausea and irritation of the nasal tract in pregnant women who are said to have used essential oils.

How About Animals?

Yes and no. Essential oils can be used in limitation on dogs such as using a certain oil to help get rid of ticks, fleas etc. But these oils are not to be used with cats, as they can develop skin irritation and can also be extremely toxic. No pet should be allowed to ingest these, as it might harm them.

Chapter 2:

Benefits of Essential Oils

Essential oils are full of benefits and in this chapter, we look at some them.

Benefits in Skincare

Fairness

Essential oils are known to promote fairness. In fact, oils such as sandalwood and rose oil can help a person in getting rid of a tan and going a couple of shades lighter. Another great oil to help lighten skin is lemon essential oil, as it contains natural bleaching agents. And if bleaching is a bit too much for you, then you can opt for a combination of olive and jojoba oil, as they can help in lightening the pigmentation and can also help with reducing tan. For sunburns, a thick application of coconut oil is said to be the best solution.

Youth

Most women in their 40's and 50's crave to have back the same kind of skin that they had, when they were younger. And with the use of essential oils, that can be a possibility. Oils such as geranium and rosehip oil help in reducing the wrinkles on face and help in getting rid fine lines. A little vitamin e oil mixed with these two oils can also help in removing laughter lines and other such expressions, which might be causing a women's face to develop lines and wrinkles.

Glow

Several essential oils are used to add a glow to the face. Especially in this day and age of excessive pollution, it becomes essential for people to take care of their skin, lest they end up with dull and damaged skin. One of the best essential oils to use in order to gain a youthful glow is almond oil and lavender oil. Both these oils help in removing any impurities from the skin and also help in increasing the number of healthy cells.

Moisture

Essential oils can be used to add moisture to the skin. Extremes of temperature, such as exposure to the heat of summer or the cold of winter, can cause our skins to dry out and it becomes important for us to provide our skins with adequate moisture. Carrot seed oil is said to be extremely moisturizing, and a little oil can go a long way in making skin soft, supple and healthy.

Benefits in Hair Care

Hair Fall

Hair fall is becoming more and more common these days, owing to excessive pollution and unhealthy lifestyles. One of the best oils to use in order to combat hair fall is coconut oil. The oil is said to help in preventing split ends and breakage, which can cause hair to fall out. Another beneficial hair oil is jojoba oil, which is loaded with vitamin e and can help in reversing hair fall to a large extent.

It also helps in thickening existing hair and preventing them from falling out.

Grey Hair

Essential oils can help in eliminating grey hair. Mustard seed oil mixed with a little castor oil and applied daily can effectively eliminate white hair and cause any discolored hair to go back to black.

Dandruff

Dandruff is a problem, which can leave you quite embarrassed. To effectively fight away dandruff, you can mix together peppermint oil, menthol oil and rosemary oil and apply it all over the scalp. It is sure to provide you with an instant relief and also help you maintain a cool scalp.

Shine

To add shine to dull and lifeless hair, you can massage it with some almond oil. Almond oil is famous for adding a unique sheen to the scalp and can also be used to moisturize the scalp and make it healthy.

Medicinal Benefits

Acne

Acne Vulgaris is extremely common amongst the youth and instead of turning to chemical laden creams to get rid of the problem, you can instead apply a thin layer of neem oil over the surface of the pimple. This will go a long way in helping to remove the bacteria that cause spots and also effectively prevent them from coming back. Tea tree oil is also as effective in treating acne and can also help get rid of acne scars. Lemon oil can be used as an astringent, to help close up open pores.

Viral

Eucalyptus oil has anti-viral properties and can be used to treat viral infections of the skin. It can also be used to treat viral infections of the scalp.

Fungal

Fungal infections such as athlete's foot and ringworms can be fought with the help of lavender oil. Just a little application can go a long way in not just helping with the symptoms but in eliminating the condition entirely.

Best Known Essential Oils in the Beauty World

In this segment, I shed some light on the best-known essential oils in the world.

Rose

Rose oil is regarded as being one of the best essential oils in the world. Most popular for its pleasant fragrance, the oil is a favorite amongst women, who use it for its therapeutic values. Rose oil is extracted from rose flowers, more so from the petals. It is a fact that each different color of rose produces a different fragrance. Rose oil is best used in cosmetics, perfumes and a little oil dabbed on the lower stomach is said to help provide relief from period cramps.

Geranium

Geranium is the second most preferred essential oil in the world. It is extremely popular with women, for helping in reducing wrinkles, fine lines and other such age related problems. The oil is extracted from the geranium plant and is in huge demand, owing to being used by several of the cosmetic industry giants.

The oil produces a certain heat, which can cause a person to gain relief from joint aches and pains. It is best known for its use in relieving varicose veins. The oil is also said to help in hair growth, as it helps in increasing the blood circulation in the scalp.

Lemon Oil

Lemon oil is extremely easy to extract but one of the most powerful of essential oils. The oil is best used as an astringent, to help close open pores in the skin. It also finds its use in bleaching the skin and helps in removing tan.

Its antibacterial properties make it one of the most preferred oils to treat acne and other bacterial infections of the skin and scalp. The oil also helps in relieving tensions and stress and can be used in making candles.

Lavender Oil

The lavender flower is one of the most sought after in the world of aromatherapy. Its benefits range in the hundreds and just a single drop is enough to help a person feel a sense of extreme calm. The oil is extensively used in cosmetics, owing to its skin healing powers. It is also used as a tincture, to help cure burns. I am sure you are aware of its application in bathroom fresheners and Potpourri.

Lavender scented candles are sold worldwide, and are extensively used in spas and beauty parlors, to help with stress and tensions. The oil can also be used in removing wrinkles and a little application over on the wrists and other pulse points, helps in establishing a soft and lingering fragrance.

Sandalwood Oil

Despite being one of the most expensive oils in the world, sandal wood oil is regarded as being one of the best skin care oils. The oil is extracted from the bark of the sandal wood tree, which is native to several Asian countries. A single bark of this wood can cost you a few hundred dollars and so, the oil is of extreme value.

The oil is best known for its use in reducing wrinkles and lines and is also used to induce a sense of calm. Sandal wood oil is used to make incense sticks which, when burned, can cause a person to sleep deeply and soundly.

Tea Tree Oil

Tea tree oil is popular for its medicinal properties. It imparts a very strong and sharp odor, and is best used in treating skin conditions. It is used in treating acne and a little can be applied to help get rid of acne Vulgaris. It is also used to treat adult acne, which can be hereditary. Its anti-bacterial properties makes it great to be used as a rash cleaner and diaper rashes can be eliminated with this oil.

Chapter 3:

Essential Oils for Relaxation

Most essential oils are used for their ability in inducing a sense of calm. These oils are effective in helping a person combat stress and tensions and also help in inducing sleep.

In this chapter, we look at how you can gain a sense of calm, by using these essential oils.

Process of Relaxation

Given our hectic lifestyles, we are often left with the need for a relaxing head massage or something that will help us beat the stress. In such a case, it is best to turn to essential oils. These oils help, not just help in relieving stress, but to beat conditions such as anxiety and depression.

These two conditions arise, when a person undergoes immense stress and the brain starts to produce excessive cortisol. Cortisol is the chemical that causes a person to have bad feelings and worry needlessly. In order to beat this chemical, the brain is supposed to produce a good one known as serotonin.

Serotonin is the happiness hormone, which helps in driving stress away and helps a person relax. Now, to force the brain to produce more serotonin and effectively cut down on the cortisol, essential oils are to be used.

These oils have the capacity of causing the mind to produce excess serotonin. They have the tendency of altering brain process and making a person feel calm and happy. Therefore, these oils are used in massage creams, massage oils, candles, Potpourri etc.

Here, we look at some of the oils best suited for stress relief.

Lavender

Lavender is the number one essential oil used for relaxation. Virtually the whole plant is used – flowers, stems and leaves – and are steam distilled. It has a distinctive aroma and is often used in bath oils and sleep aids as well as in massage oils and is one of the very few that can be used neat, without a carrier oil. Lavender's properties include antibacterial, analgesic, anti-inflammatory, decongestant, antifungal and calming as well as balancing and anti-anxiety, making it one of the most versatile oils all round.

Sandalwood

Sandalwood is an ancient essential oil, with its roots deep in Indian medicine. It is high in something called sesquiterpenes, which are responsible for stimulation of the pineal gland. This gland relaxes the nervous system and that's why Sandalwood is used in meditation. And, because the gland also releases melatonin, it aids a deep and restful sleep and Sandalwood is a common oil found in sleep remedies. Its properties include, among other things, antidepressant, immune stimulant, antiseptic, sedative, tonic.

Bergamot

Bergamot is another preferred essential oil to help relieve stress. It is derived from a citrus plant that produces lemon like fruits. The scent is mild and citrusy and is used for topical application. It is best used in massage oils and also be used to make aromatherapy candles. The best way to use this oil is to apply a drop over the forehead and massage it in. you can also use it to add to your bath water. This oil is safe for consumption and can be added to food as well. Bergamot contains antidepressant, digestive and analgesic properties as well as antispasmodic and antidepressant.

Cedar Wood

Cedar wood is extremely effective in calming a busy mind. In fact, this is the only oil that is said to help children with Attention Deficit Hyperactive Disorder, or ADHD. The oil has also been proven to promote sleep and a small amount is enough for a person to gain a sound sleep. The best place to apply this oil is at the stem of the neck behind the head, where the neck ends and the head starts. A small drop can be placed in the area and massaged thoroughly. The properties contained in Cedar Wood essential oil are antiseptic, diuretic, anti-fungal and antiseptic as well as the sedative properties that make it ideal for relaxation

Chamomile

Chamomile is a flower whose essential oil is extensively used to provide relief from stress and beat insomnia. One of the main causes for stress, these days, is emotional instability and so, by applying a little chamomile oil over the forehead, a person can garner control over their emotions. The oil is powerful enough to send a person into a state of trance, where he or she gains the same benefits as with meditation. The best area to apply this oil is the over the throat. A small drop can be placed on the palm, and the palm can be rubbed over the throat. Chamomile contains a very large number of properties, including antidepressant, anti-neuralgic, analgesic, anti-inflammatory, anti-infectious, and digestive amongst many others, which go to making it one of the most calming essential oils.

Frankincense

This oil is used to clear a cloudy mind. For people who get angry for no reason or are always confused, then this oil can do a sea of good. The oil penetrates through the skin and mixes with the blood stream. It then travels to the brain and has the capacity of altering brain function. It helps in removing any blockages and barriers and allows a person to think rationally. The oil is best applied on the forehead and even better is to burn some frankincense and inhale its powerful fumes. The health benefits and properties of Frankincense are antiseptic, expectorant, tonic, digestive, diuretic and sedative, amongst others.

Marjoram

Marjoram is an herb that has been in use since ancient times. It was known as "the herb of happiness" owing to its tendency of making a person happy. The herb is used to treat insomnia and allow a person to garner a good night's sleep. A little oil applied to the sides of the temple and massaged in, can cause a person to not just have a good night's sleep but also help in combating headaches and migraine. Properties include analgesic, diuretic, stomachic, expectorant, fungicidal, digestive and antispasmodic as well as being a nervine, which is where its calming and relaxation properties come from.

Neroli

Neroli is a type of citrus oil that is known to promote confidence. It's steam distilled from bitter-orange flowers and is very expensive, being that it can take up to 450 kg of blossom to make 1 lb. of the oil. It is an effective treatment against anxiety and asleep disorders that arise from shock, emotional issues and anxiety. You don't need too much of it, a little oil can go a long way in eliminating stress, depression and anxiety and promoting self- confidence. Active properties include anti-anxiety, antiseptic, tissue stimulant, and antidepressant amongst others.

Chapter 4:

DIY Cosmetics for You to Try Out

Before you get down to making these cosmetics, I would like to run you through the process of making your own oils.

This is an explanation of the distiller method but you can also extract oils in other methods that you think is best suited for your needs.

To make a distiller, you will need the following.

- A pressure cooker
- A long rubber pipe
- A small metal pipe (cut to fit the steam valve of the cooker)
- A tub of water
- Lavender flowers
- Water
- Collecting jar

Method

1. Place the cooker on the stove and fill it with thoroughly washed lavender flowers.
2. You can add in a few stems for enhanced flavor.

3. Add the water into it such that it completely covers the flowers to the brim.

4. Close the lid and attach the metal pipe to the steam valve.

5. To the open end, attach the rubber pipe and coil it.

6. Place the coiled bit in a tub containing cold water and the open end needs to go into a collecting jar.

7. Place the cooker on high heat and wait for the water to come to a boil.

8. You will slowly start to notice that the collection jar is filling up.

9. Allow it to boil for 3 hours or until you are satisfied with the amount collected.

10. Now place it in a cool dark room and allow the oil to skim to the top of the water.

11. You can extract the oil and place it in small bottles.

12. Your lavender essential oil is ready to use but is best left for 48 hours to mature.

Oils to Aid Relaxation

These are some of the best oil blends to help you relax and let your worries take flight.

Calming Diffuser

Ingredients

- 18 drops Lavender essential oil
- 15 drops Rosewood essential oil
- 12 drops Chamomile essential oil
- 12 drops Geranium essential oil
- 10 drops Clary Sage essential oil
- 10 drops Ylang Ylang essential oil
- 8 Drops Marjoram essential oil

Method

1. Place all of the oils into a small glass container and shake it well to blend them together
2. Add a few drops to a diffuser, in the bedroom, lounge or bathroom and enjoy the relaxing experience
3. Relaxing Bath Oil
4. Ingredients
5. 4 drops Chamomile essential oil
6. 2 drops Lavender essential oil

Method

1. Add the oils to a warm bath, under the running water so they disperse through the bath
2. Enjoy just before bedtime for a relaxing sleep

Comforting Spray

Ingredients

- 8 drops Lavender essential oil
- 3 drops Vanilla essential oil (or 30 if you use the Vanilla in Jojoba oil)
- 3 drops Ylang Ylang essential oil
- 10 drops Orange essential oil
- 8 drops Cedar Wood essential oil
- ½ teaspoon of emulsifier
- 2 oz. distilled water

Method

1. Add all of the oils to the emulsifier and shake well
2. Add the water, shake to blend and spray around the room
3. Relaxing Pillow Spray
4. Ingredients
5. 15 ml distilled water
6. 2 drops of Lavender essential oil
7. 1 drop Chamomile essential oil
8. 1 drop Orange essential oil
9. 1 drop Ylang Ylang essential oil

Method

1. Blend all the ingredients together
2. Spray on pillowcases for a deep and relaxing sleep

Oils to Beat Stress

Here, we will look at some of the best oil combinations to help you beat stress.

Rejuvenating Oil

Ingredients

- 10 drops Chamomile essential oil
- 10 drops lavender essential oil
- 10 drops Vetiver essential oil
- 10 drops bergamot essential oil

Method

1. To prepare this oil, you can extract each one using the distiller method or buy them from a store.
2. Place all the oils in a small bottle and shake it to mix well.
3. Make sure that the bottle has a spray attachment.
4. Spray a little on your pulse points and rub it a little.
5. This will help you forget your stress and help you relax.

Sleep Inducing Oil

Ingredients

- 10 drops Ylang Ylang essential oil
- 10 drops Neroli essential oil
- 10 drops frankincense essential oil
- 10 drops rose essential oil

Method

1. Mix all ingredients and place in a spray bottle.
2. This mix can be used to spray on palm and smelt just before retiring to bed.
3. It can also be directly sprayed over the pillowcase or the mattress.
4. This oil is also suitable to be added to bath water.

Creams And Soap

Forehead Massage Cream

Ingredients

- 10 drops flax seed oil
- 10 drops lavender essential oil
- 10 drops sandal wood essential oil
- 10 drops lemon essential oil
- 5 drops vitamin E oil
- 1 cup Shea butter

Method

1. Start by preparing a double boiler and melting the Shea butter to a consistency of your choice.

2. You can then add in the rest of the oils and give it a good mix.

3. Use an electric blender to whip the butter to reach a fluffy consistency.

4. Your massage oil is ready and when applied to the forehead, it is sure to drive all you stress and tensions away.

Aromatherapy Body/ Foot/ Hand Soap

Ingredients

- 2 cups clear glycerin soap base
- 10 drops tea tree oil
- 10 drops rose oil
- 10 drops lavender oil
- 10 drops rosemary oil
- ½ cup fresh lemon rind
- Soap mold or ice cube trays

Method

1. Melt the glycerin soap base using a double boiler system.
2. Once it melts, add in the oils and give it a good mix.
3. Pour it into the molds or the ice cube trays.
4. You can now add the rind equally and use a toothpick to push it in.
5. Allow it to set for 24 hours.
6. Your soaps are ready to use and they can help you in having a calm and relaxing bath.

Relaxing Hair Oil

Ingredients

- ½ cup coconut oil
- 10 drops almond essential oil
- 10 drops jasmine essential oil
- 10 drops vitamin e oil

Method

1. Mix all the oils in a bowl and transfer it to a bottle.
2. Use it to massage the hair and scalp.

Candle and Potpourri

Lavender Candle

Ingredients

- 1 normal candle
- 20 drops lavender essential oil
- Violet food color

Method

1. Cut the candle into small pieces and save the wick from the center.
2. Place the pieces in a double boiler and allow it to completely melt.

3. Once it does, add in the oil and mix well.

4. Add in the food color and mix until evenly combined.

5. Pour it into a mold of your choice and insert a small wick in the center.

6. This candle is sure to help you have a very relaxing bath/ sleep/ leisure time.

Orange And Rose Potpourri

Ingredients

- 1 cup dried rose petals
- 1 cup dried lavender flowers
- ½ cup dried twigs (cinnamon preferably)
- 10 drops orange essential oil
- 10 drops rose essential oil

Method

1. Place the dried leaves and twigs in a small bowl and mix it together.
2. Add in the oils and give it a good mix.
3. Place it in a fancy bowl and place the bowl in the center of the room.
4. The Potpourri will help in spreading a fine fragrance.

Conclusion

I thank you once again for purchasing this Book and hope you enjoyed reading it.

The main aim of this book was to give you a fair idea of what essential oils are all about and what you can do with them. As is apparent from the book, essential oils are extracted from seeds, barks, plants, herbs etc. and can be bought from a store or made at home.

We learnt of the various benefits of these oils and also looked at six of the best essential oils in the world of beauty and looked at the various ways in which these oils can provide us with relaxing benefits and the best-suited plants for the same.

Finally, we looked at a lot of the cosmetics and other accessories that you can easily make at home and put these oils to best use.

I hope to have inspired you to start making your own oils and use it to make some skin and hair care products.

Here's to wishing you luck with all your endeavors!

Good luck!

Essential Oils

3rd Edition

Essential Oils as Natural Medicine

Holistic Herbal Remedies and Recipes for Common Ailments

Introduction

Health is one of the most important factors in living a fulfilling life. However, people tend to disregard its importance in their daily lives. They spend most of their time trying to earn money and continually push their health off until later days, without seeing that life is so much more than that. The stressors that people subject themselves to are enormous. Thus, it's more important that people look after their bodies and their mental health on a regular basis to ensure they are operating at their peak capacity. Many things that can be used to ease stress and promote health are expensive treatments or time consuming practices, but essential oils can be used to help you to achieve balance within your life without taking up a large amount of your time and money.

It's a well-known fact that stress and tension are the main reasons why people suffer from many of the health issues that could be avoided. If you can control the amount of stress that you are suffering from, then chances are that you won't suffer as many physical ailments. One efficient way to tackle stress and other related physical disorders is to learn how to use essential oils. These have been used for centuries and are established as a means to help people to relax and to feel physically better.

When you learn the different uses of essential oils, you can treat a variety of diseases or even treat symptoms that may later turn to problematic disorders without having to revert to pharmaceutical solutions. Although herbal medicine may be viewed as being a very "in" thing, essential oils have been used for centuries by many cultures as a primary method of treating physical ailments. They have helped many generations to feel better and to maximize the benefits derived from them.

This book is written with the intention of helping you to learn all about essential oils, their uses and their benefits. The knowledge contained in the book should give you sufficient impetus to start making the use of essential oils something that comes as second nature.

Thank you for purchasing this Book and hope you will find the information contained within its chapters helpful and useful in conquering ailments, diseases and health problems. It is also hoped that tradition will be kept alive and that you will pass your knowledge on to your family members and friends.

Chapter 1:

What are Essential Oils?

Before understanding the qualities as well as the uses of Essential Oils, it is necessary to understand what exactly they are. Mother Nature has been very generous, in that each plant is given different elements which can be used in a variety of ways. One of these is the aroma. Another part of a plant may be that part which produces oils. The oils that are extracted from these plants are known to have health benefits. Essential oils provide instant relief from many ailments and can help individuals looking for solutions that are not pharmaceutical, but rather derived from nature.

These oils are extracted from areas of the plant such as the flower tips or indeed berries or leaves. A fine example of this is lavender. Known for its therapeutic values, the aroma of lavender is extracted to make oil which gives the user a strong sense of well-being. There are various methods of extraction, which include steam distillation, cold pressing. A true essential oil will contain no other content but that which is taken from the plant. Its composition is fairly thick in consistency but rarely sticky.

It's important to realize that many manufacturers use these oils and try to "enhance" what nature has offered, though the results are not as effective as pure essential oils. These may be laced with chemicals to make the oils look more acceptable or to enhance the scent of the oils. Besides coming from a plant and being, in effect, vegetation produced by products, essential oils are more than that. They contain very important and potent ingredients from nature itself. Thus, you can expect a pure essential oil to have contents which include aromatic properties, such as in the case of eucalyptus and lavender. They can also have very therapeutic ingredients within the same plant, meaning that their uses are diverse. For example, eucalyptus may be suited to use to help breathing when suffering from a cough. It also has agents which can help in the healing process for muscle tiredness.

Common Sources of Essential Oils

Thus it can be seen that essential oils are those oils extracted from plants and that their pureness helps in the therapeutic process. Common plants used for their beneficial properties are lavender, Clary sage, basil, eucalyptus, bergamot, rose, germanium, vetiver lemon, chamomile, frankincense, grapefruit, neroli, marjoram, spearmint, juniper, clove, peppermint and ylang ylang.

Think of peeling an orange. Think of the zest of the aroma which is released during that process and you will begin to understand what an essential oil is. This zest from the peel is cold pressed to produce the oils that people recognize as essential oils.

As essential oils are non-sticky fluids they need to be mixed with carrier oils. Various good quality oils like almond oil, sesame oil, carrot seed oil, coconut oil etc. are used as carrier oils.

Essential oils should always be pure. These will be grown and harvested by companies who then extract the oils and will sell them through outlets to customers who are looking for help from nature. For example, a typical essential oil used for massage is that which is extracted from the Bergamot fruit. In this case, the oil is obtained by cold pressing the skin of the fruit. As you can imagine, this means that the oil is precious and fairly expensive, though the health benefits are enormous. Used for massage therapy and for skin care, the price compared with commercial pharmaceutical products is a reasonable one without all the potential of causing harm. The nature of aromatherapy is that the ingredients themselves have gone through a standardized process which means that none of the goodness is lost.

Did you know that essential oils can be produced from seeds? Indeed they can. The cardamom seed is a very powerful seed used for producing essential oils. This seed is commonly used in Indian cuisine, though in oil format can be beneficial for the digestion, as well as being extremely powerful in helping people to breathe better.

Even the wood from a tree can be used to produce essential oils. Have you ever experienced how cedar wood smells? You may have noticed this at Christmas when the

Christmas tree is in the home for a length of time. However, the oils extracted from this element of nature are known to be beneficial for many common ailments.

Essential oils are oils produced from nature. It's as simple as that, although the process of extraction is complex and takes on many different forms. Companies accustomed to producing these oils have no need to add "goodness" because the oils themselves have sufficient goodness all on their own. That's what makes them essential to healthy living.

The Origin of Essential Oils

Many people wonder when people began to use essential oils and there's quite a history behind the use of oils in healing. Plants have been used in this way for thousands of years and recorded use of oils can be found to be linked to Roman and early Egyptian times. René-Maurice Gattefosse may not be a name that you are familiar with, although you will certainly be familiar with the name that he gave to the use of essential oils in his writings on the subject of "aromatherapy" after realizing the potential that plant oils had in healing.

Everyone has heard of aromatherapy these days, though the essential oils that we use today have had all the hard work taken out of the production process. Companies now produce these using traditional methods and the small bottle of oil that you see on the shelf of your pharmacy or store has a whole wealth of history, worthwhile reading about because it is the story of discovery and one which means that essential oils are available for everyone in this day and age. The production of these oils back in Roman times may have differed slightly though the remedial effects of using the oils were well known back then. That means that essential oils are oils that mankind finds "essential" for keeping the body in good form.

Chapter 2:

Why Essential Oils are Better than Other Medicines

You may have wondered why essential oils are indeed better than modern medicines in some cases of day to day illnesses. There are many reasons, although you will see from this chapter that they may not always be obvious ones. Essential oils are not harmful to the body. They do not have the side effects of modern medicines. If you were to take a packet of regular medication from the pharmacy and read the details which come with it, you will find a whole host of secondary side effects which "may" be experienced. The fact is that people react to different medications in different ways. Although they have been tested by the FDA as safe, there are still lists and lists of side effects that can be suffered as a consequence of taking medication.

Essential Oils are good value

The investment in a set of essential oils means that you have a medicine cabinet right in your home for times when help is needed. Although of course you may need to get help from a doctor or at least ask for the doctor's reassurance on certain conditions, once you get accustomed to the use of essential oils, you will find that you won't need as much medical treatment and that you won't be filling out expensive prescriptions so often.

Be sure to look on the bottle of essential oils to ensure that no other ingredients have been added. These are available over the counter, but there are different grades and cheaper oils may just be cheap because they have been mixed with other ingredients. Remember also that it's not how pretty the bottles are that counts. The main thing to remember when buying your kit is that they are pure oils.

No Side Effects

Essential oils come from natural and herbal sources, as they are derived from plant and natural sources. If these oils are used holistically and under proper supervision, no harm is caused whatsoever. As compared to pharmaceutical drugs, essential oils have relatively zero harmful side effects. Even prolonged use of essential oils will not cause any harm, unlike regular drugs.

Although these oils do not have any side effects, it is necessary to check whether you are allergic to any oil before using it. Allergies should always be taken into account when using any product to help your health, just the same as when you are choosing food.

If you are allergic to natural elements, then it's quite possible that you will be allergic to the oils associated with those natural elements and should avoid using that particular oil. However, other oils may be very beneficial to you in your health regime.

Market Availability

Unlike regular medicines, essential oils are available easily, either over the counter or through an Internet website. They can also be bought from a variety of stores and not just drug stores. Essential oils do not require prescriptions and can be bought easily. You can even grow your own herbs and extract oils from them if you feel you have the patience. This is one reason why essential oils are one of the most popular alternative forms of medicine throughout the world. In olden days, the oils would be extracted by your ancestors, following study of how certain species of plants seemed to help animals. Nowadays, their uses are well known and documented and the essential oils are available worldwide regardless of what the natural flora and fauna of a particular country are. The spread of aromatherapy has been a consequence of this availability.

For use in the case of chronic illnesses

Many chronic diseases like arthritis and chronic aches and pains require prolonged use of drugs. These disorders do not always respond well to regular drugs. Prolonged use of modern drugs is not advised, as these drugs may cause harmful side-effects. If you look at illnesses such as arthritis, for example, one may be prescribed anti-inflammatory drugs to try and reduce inflammation. This is of course the natural way to treat the illness. However, anti-inflammatory drugs may have unwanted side effects and often more drugs are prescribed to counter those side effects. It's a vicious circle and one that chronically ill people find hard to cope with.

These kinds of chronic illnesses need good, holistic medicines, which won't cause any harm even after prolonged use. Thus, essential oils are better suited for treating such illnesses. The better part is that such disorders also respond well to being treated with essential oils. As these oils are easy to use they are highly recommended for those who have to suffer the indignity of chronic illness or pain.

Safety

A variety of modern drugs use components derived from natural ingredients like plant sources. Many drugs contain essential oil extracts. So why not go fully natural and use just essential oils instead of risking the side-effects that come as part and parcel of modern medicine?

Essential oils have been used for thousands of years throughout the world. The ancient Egyptians, Indians, Chinese and even the Romans used essential oils as herbal remedies for all kinds of ailments. Since these oils are tried and tested and their knowledge has been passed down generation to generation, they could be considered as a safe alternative to modern medicine.

Multiple Benefits

Unlike regular medicines, essential oils do not pinpoint a specific disease or disorder. Quite often, essential oils, used with an intention of curing one disorder can hone in on other ailments that the user suffers from. So essential oils have multiple benefits and thus are far better than the regular medicines which are prescribed for a specific ailment. Examples could be that breathing is improved as a side consequence of using an essential oil for inflammation or digestive problems. Thus, the benefits are enormous and the impact of using essential oils can be life changing.

Apart than this, essential oils pack hefty amounts of essential nutrients, which are required by the human body. As these nutrients come from natural sources you need not worry whether they will cause any side effects. You do not need to buy artificial food supplements to make up for deficiencies in the body.

The Benefit of Detoxing the Body

One of the major reasons for the rise in illnesses is the increasing amount of toxicity that human beings expose themselves to. Air and water pollution causes harmful toxins to enter their bodies, which lead to many different ailments and problems. To get rid of these toxins it is necessary to detoxify the body.

With today's fast lives, desk jobs and extra working hours, a lot of people are prone to stress which, in turn, makes way for other physiological problems. Essential oils are one of the best remedies for stress management. These oils can help people to detoxify their minds and bodies and help them to relax.

You may have heard of the benefits of detoxing and have probably seen many products which purport to help the body to detoxify. However, some have risks and others are purely speculative. Essential oils, however, are proven to work and can help the body recover from all that modern day life throws at it. When you get to use essential oils and begin to reap the benefits, there will be no doubt left in your mind as to the efficiency of essential oils to help the body get back into shape.

Prevention Is Better Than Cure

As the famous adage goes "prevention is better than cure." Essential oils are the perfect solution not just to cure ailments but to prevent them from recurring. Unlike regular medicines, essential oils have immunity boosting powers, which help you in preventing diseases.

You can use essential oils even when you are not ill to keep your body safe and healthy without any side effects. How does this help? The way that the aromas work is that there are certain aromas which help human beings to feel well. Imagine the scent of roses. Imagine the aroma of sage or coriander. Feel how ginger helps digestion and how mint helps the body to breathe well even though these may not actually be caused by illness. Habits such as smoking can cause the lungs and the bronchial passages to be blocked and essential oils can put that right and make the user feel the advantages straight away.

If you have ever walked into a room and been greeted with an odor which was pleasant, you will know how this felt. Common aromas which help wellbeing are aromas such as Lemongrass, Lime and Marjoram. Each of these essential oils helps you to feel stimulated mentally and at peace with your body.

The power of essential oils, once released can help so many aspects of health, from helping skin to heal or to feel a glow to helping the hair to look sleek and shiny, essential oils release their goodness into the atmosphere and you instantly feel the benefit that is derived from them.

The balance of hormones can be achieved by the use of Ylang Ylang essential oils. Wild Orange helps to purify the skin and reinforce the immunity system. There are so many hidden benefits that these are hard to describe in a full way. The reason for this is that nature has a way of producing help from unexpected places and the benefits of one essential oil can be for so many different aspects of life. The example of Wild Orange can be used as a typical dual purpose or even triple purpose essential oil, being used for the skin, the immunity system and also to protect the body from the seasonal changes in the atmosphere and weather. This one essential oil also invigorates and helps to refresh mind and body, meaning that you don't just use it when you are ill.

You use essential oils for prevention and that is something that can be incorporated into your life, so that illnesses do not become such a pressure upon you. Prevention is indeed much wiser than waiting until a disease needs a cure.

Chapter 3:

How to Determine the Quality of Essential Oils?

Certified Pure Therapeutic Grade Oils

You've probably heard of aromatherapy, right? Maybe tried it for yourself, even. You might have heard from people that they didn't think it was all that great. It could be that you tried it yourself and weren't too satisfied with it. What went wrong?

Simple, you used the wrong oils.

In aromatherapy, it was important that the quality of the oils is up to par, and to ensure this, a system of grading has been developed. Medicinal aromatherapy has great potential for health benefits. It can make you feel younger, full of vigor, and improve your lifestyle in a variety of ways. However, for it to work to its full potential, you need to make sure that what you're working with lives up to the standards and are of a good quality.

The problem here lies in the fact that almost 98% of the production of essential oils is not intended for serious aromatherapy. Most of it is produced for the fragrance, cosmetic and culinary industries. Still, a lot of marketers try to dupe customers and sell these oils in the name of aromatherapy oils. If serious aromatherapy, and not of the recreational kind is performed with these oils, you will end up experiencing dissatisfaction.

The aroma of a good grade essential oil should be strong- not overpowering, but potent. The aroma should be deep, rich and complex, making it a good complement for therapeutic chemicals. CPTG oils do not irritate the skin, and lift the body's frequency.

Certified Pure Therapeutic Grade or CPTG is a trademark that helps in achieving a standard of essential oils that are fit for use. CPTG oil has a rich aroma, is kinetically active and helps rejuvenate and lift the frequency of the human body. Fragrance, chemistry and frequency are components used to determine production standards, and if the oil lacks in one of these areas, it cannot be called CPTG.

Production of a truly therapeutic-grade oil

Since the composition of a quality essential oil is so complex, chemically, the key to preparing these essential oils is to make sure that as many aromatic compounds as possible are preserved within the oil. Aromatic compounds are quite fragile, so it can be tricky to extract them. For an oil to be extracted properly, a certain level of knowledge and skill is required, along with sufficient time and patience. Great care must be taken during production, keeping the following aspects in mind:

Growing plants of the proper variety
Selecting the species is a very important step, since various plants produce oils of different qualities. Cultivars need to ensure that

the species that render the best quality of essential oils are selected for cultivation. For example, lavender oil extracted from an authentic Lavandula Augustifolia plant is low in camphor, and rich in the constituents that lend lavender its therapeutic properties, such as lavendulol and lavendulol acetate.

Usage of proper cultivation processes

Plants grown for extraction of essential oils should be cultivated on uncontaminated, virgin lands, free of pesticides, fungicides, herbicides and other chemical fertilizers. Agrochemicals are prone to reacting with essential oils during the distillation process. So it is important that the plants do not interact with agrochemicals. Pesticides are generally soluble in oil, so there is a risk of them mixing with the oil. Such toxic chemicals are transferred to the body if diffused or topically applied, and lead to bad results.

The location of cultivation of such plants should be sufficiently far from polluted areas such as factories, nuclear plants, or highly populated cities. The soil used for growing these plants should be conditioned well with organic bio-solids and trace minerals, as plants lacking in these lead to production of oils low in therapeutic value.

Mountain water is the most ideal for watering of these plants. Municipality treated water, or runoff water must be avoided at all costs as they contain harmful chemicals that will deplete the quality of these plants.

Harvesting with proper knowledge and skill

Timing of the harvest is a vital factor in determining the quality of the oil- if harvested at the wrong time of year; it can lead to production of an essential oil which is sub-standard in quality. In a few cases, harvesting at the wrong hour of the day might even make a huge difference. For example, German chamomile yields more azulene if harvested in the morning than it would if picked in the late afternoon. Timing is key!

Other factors that should be considered while harvesting include the percentage of plant in bloom, the quantity of dew gathered on the leaves, the condition of the climate during the two weeks before the harvest. Transportation time should be decreased, as there is a risk of pollutants, mold and dust affecting the herbs. For convenience, distillers should be located close to the harvesting area.

Proper extraction of the oils

Later in the book, you will learn about the methods of extraction used to produce essential oils. These methods include, but are not limited to solvent extraction, steam distillation, and carbon dioxide extraction. Now, extraction is a very tricky proper, and it demands to be handled with extreme care. Distillation is an art, and minor differences in the equipment and processing conditions may lead to irreparable differences in the quality of the essential oil. There are a few factors that have to be kept in mind during distillation, and these include temperature, pressure, size of each batch, the duration of time taken to process a batch, and the composition of the equipments used.

Aromatic compounds may be destroyed if the temperature varies a little higher than ideal. Distillation processes must employ low-temperature methods so as to preserve the oil's pH and electropositive balance. Similarly, when it comes to pressure, high pressure should be avoided. It alters the pH of the essential oil and induces harshness in the oil. It is very important that the distillation is allowed to go on for the sufficient amount of time, no less and no more. The time required for the distillation of various essential oils differs greatly, ranging from an hour and half for lavender, to about 24 hours for cypress. It is advised to not let the oils come in contact with chemically reactive metals. A CPTG essential oil must be distilled in a cooking chamber made of food-grade stainless steel. Also, the batch size of the essential oils should be small.

Testing of the oils at independent labs

Even after ensuring that the cultivation, harvesting and processing are done properly, it is still prudent to check the quality of the oils through careful testing performed in independent laboratories. This is the best way to clarify whether or not an essential oil is truly Certified Pure Therapeutic Grade or not. The oils that do not meet the stringent requirements are rejected and not classified as CPTG.

Tests undertaken to ensure CPTG quality:

Once you know the properties that constitute a good quality essential oil, it becomes clear what to test the oils on the basis of, in order to determine their quality. Companies producing essential oils need to look at their production with the perception of medical individuals; they need to ensure that these oils yield the maximum health benefits as possible.

The following are a list of tests conducted to verify whether or not an oil is CPTG in quality.

Gas Chromatography

Once the aromatic compounds are extracted and distilled from the plant carefully, samples are gathered for their chemical composition, by employing the method of gas chromatography. In this method, vaporization of volatile essential oil compounds is done, and then passed through a long column. This column is known as a chromatograph. Every individual compound of the oil travels at a different rate in the column, and is measured as the compound exits the column during testing. By using the method of gas chromatography, the individuals responsible for determining the compounds present in a test sample can easily tell their levels and composition.

Mass Spectrometry

In this method, the samples for testing are first vaporized and then ionized. Then, the weight of each compound in the sample in weighed. The objective of mass spectrometry is to provide insight into how pure the essential oil really is, and reveal the presence of non-aromatic compounds, too heavy to travel alongside in a gas chromatograph. Gas chromatography and mass spectrometry are combined and known as the GC/MS test sometimes.

Fourier Transform Infrared Spectroscopy

Also referred to as the FTIR scan method, this entails a scan similar to the GC/MS testing. Samples of essential oil are transported to the facility where the manufacturing takes place, for filling. Before the samples are released into the facility, the batch to be tested is quarantined while other tests are performed on it. One of them is the FTIR scan, in which, light is directed at the sample, and then the amount absorbed by the compounds present in the oil is measured. By rallying the results against a database, composition standards are determined and judged.

Microbial Testing

It is important to check the essential oils for any fungus, mold or other bio-hazards. Before releasing the batch of oils from quarantine, into manufacturing, microbial testing is performed on them. In this method, samples are taken from the batch and applied on growing mediums on plates, or in dishes. Once they have passed the incubation period, each dish is checked for the growth of microbes. This test is performed uniformly on all material that makes it to the manufacturing facility, and then on the final product to make sure that no harmful microbes have contaminated the product during the filling and labeling process. This is done to ensure shelf life stability.

Organoleptic Testing

This is the part of the CPTG control process where a human touch is involved. In organoleptic testing, the quality of the oil is determined on the basis of properties that can be tested on the basis of touch, smell, sight and taste. The people involved in this process vary in background; from manufacturing engineers and essential oil practitioners, to even harvesters and oil chemists. With the assistance of these people, the quality of each Certified Pure Therapeutic Grade oil is monitored. The skill and knowledge of oil experts is valuable and indispensable when it comes to maintaining the CPTG standard.

Chapter 4:

How to Use Essential Oils?

Essential oils can be used in a variety of ways and with a variety of techniques. It's worth looking at some of the most popular ways to use essential oils as incorporating their use into your life will be life enhancing and will become second nature. The use of essential oils, not just when needed, but when you feel like reaping the benefits psychologically is something that you can incorporate into your day to day life. Remember that you need a cross section of essential oils because this means that your home kit will be there when you need it or when you feel that your body needs a little pampering.

Inhalation or vaporization

One of the easiest and simplest of ways to use essential oils is by inhaling them. Essential oils can be inhaled by the use of a diffuser where the essential oils are diluted in boiling water. These are very good for intense inhalation with the use of a towel, or to simply place within the bedroom so that the air is filled with the aroma required at bedtime.

Diffusers or vaporizers, which are specifically made for aromatherapy can be bought and can be used to dilute the droplets and to keep that aroma in the room. This can be used in a child's bedroom, a bathroom (for relaxation) or in the family room so that everyone derives the benefit of the inhalation process. The amount used will vary between 6 to 10 drops, depending upon the size of the vaporizer.

If you can imagine the aroma of eucalyptus when a child has a sore throat, or the aroma of ylang ylang while a daughter is suffering period problems, then you can see how widely aromatherapy essential oils can be beneficial to everyone.

Cosmetics

Nowadays, the cosmetic market is full of products, which are thoroughly chemical based and cause more harm than benefit in long term use. Fortunately there are cosmetics that are herbal based and made using essential oils. These oils will rejuvenate your skin and make it healthier, without any harmful side-effects.

If you are going to use essential oils for your skin, then you do need to remember that it's necessary to use carrier oil. Neat essential oil is too potent and it's wise to choose a carrier oil that is as natural as possible. Dilute a couple of drops of the chosen essential oil into 10ml of carrier oil and then use the essential oil on your skin. This can be used for areas which need healing but used as a precaution against skin blemishes, the essential oils are very rich and effective.

Bathing pleasure

Baths are an easy way to use essential oils. Just lace your bath water with your favourite oils and soak in. It will calm down your senses and relax your body. This will aid you to forget all your stress and worries and thus relieve you from aches and pains. What you need to remember is that the essential oil should be added to milk or a carrier before being added to the water. Add this while the water is running and you will instantly notice the pleasant aroma.

Massage

Massage oils are often laced with aromatherapy essential oils anyway. Getting a massage purely with essential oils will allow your body to absorb the oils easily and quickly. Massage will also help you to relax and rejuvenate.

In the case of massage, the oils must of course be used with a carrier oil. You cannot use pure oils from the bottle as they may be too harsh. Remember the rule to mix your essential oils before use, as this helps to dilute the strength and at the same time will mean you will use less and get more effective results.

The above mentioned methods are the most common ways to use essential oils and it's likely that you will find that different blends of essential oils will help you to overcome problems or to prevent them. There are also creams and gels which contain essential oils and which are useful for all kinds of conditions. In the case of creams and gels, the dilution has already taken place and these are suitable to use topically.

Here is a quick look at some of the ailments and conditions that can be warded off with the use of essential oils. This list is by no means exhaustive and you may find uses yourself that help with your well-being and that are useful for members of your family. Remember, you will probably see around 40-50 different essential oils on the market, although there are of course up to 70 essential oils that are commonly known to help. The varieties of oils come in the following families: Spicy, woody, citrus, green or floral.

Here are the ailments which are commonly treated:

Diseases and disorders like heart diseases, obesity, blood pressure etc. can be controlled with the proper use of essential oils. As you can see, the scope of this section is rather wide. These would be ailments which are ongoing and which can debilitate your life. With the use of essential oils, they can be kept to minimally invasive. If you do have a heart condition, be sure to speak to your doctor before using the oils, since certain oils may provoke reactions.

Stress can be easily managed and controlled with the help of essential oils. These are calming and will help you to control your feelings of negativity. Do be aware that if you are on medications, these usually need to be weaned off rather than stopped and you do need supervision from your doctor. The problem with many modern medications for stress and depression are that they are long term medications and you cannot just stop taking them.

Essential oils are extremely beneficial for the skin and overall skin health. These can come in the form of topical creams and gels and there are specific varieties which are known to help keep the skin clear.

Insomnia and other sleep related diseases can be cured with essential oils, as they help you to calm your mind and body. If you are suffering from this, you can prepare your bedroom so that it creates a relaxing atmosphere and also take note that eating and drinking late at night may provoke sleeplessness at a time when your body needs sleep in order to heal naturally.

In the next chapter, we will take a quick look at how essential oils are extracted and how you can extract them at home if you prefer to use your own sources. Although this sounds complex, many people do this successfully and even grow their own plants for this specific purpose.

Chapter 5:

Extracting Essential Oils

It is not clear when mankind started using essential oils, but it is clear that essential oils have been in use for thousands of years. Mayan civilization and other civilizations during that era used essential oils. These oils were also popular with the medieval Mughals of India, the Arabs and Persians. Ancient Egyptians, Chinese and Indian medicines are also known to have used essential oils for the longest time and are still using them today.

Throughout the history of mankind, many different types of processes have been used to extract oils efficiently from plant sources. These different methods have been developed through the years to make the process simple, easy, more yielding and less time consuming. Thus, these are now commercially viable as well as being something that individuals with the time and the inclination can do themselves.

Many will be put off by the fact that the prices of essential oils are affordable, so why waste the energy making them? Others will see the benefits of making their own because they then know the exact ingredients and have no question about the purity of the products that they are using.

Yet, it is noteworthy that the basic methods of extraction of essential oils are still the same as they have been for centuries.

Not much has changed in the basic overview. The extraction is very important factor as the final product depends upon how well the process has been performed. Thus, the result will always be different and solely based upon the mastery of the extractor and the process, as well as the quality of the plants used. If the extractor isn't experienced enough, the quality of the oil will suffer as a consequence, though once they have learned the techniques, the quality will improve.

In modern times, we are able to buy essential oils over the counter, as they are commercially prepared. But if you want to keep the process holistic you can very easily extract essential oils at home and be sure that the products you use come completely from nature. That in itself is quite satisfying to those who are conscious of the difference between quality differences between home extracted and commercially produced oils. This is added as some oils do have dubious contents, though you should always look at the label and expect the oils that you buy to be pure, rather than mixed with anything commercial just to enhance color or aroma. Cheaper makes may not give you the "pure" oil that you think you are buying.

Extracting essential oils is not as complicated as it seems. It is also very cost effective if you frequently use essential oils and want them readily available. Although, the price of essential oils is less than modern medicines, it is still quite steep, especially you need them in large quantities. It really is an individual choice whether to use trusted brands or to make your own.

If you make essential oils at home it will cost you practically nothing and you will have your own, handmade and holistic batch of essential oils. Let us now take a look at how essential oils can be extracted at home.

The most important method for extracting essential oils is distilling so it would be beneficial for you to get cheap distillation apparatus or construct this at home. Here are some of the items you will need for distilling essential oils. Many will be things that you already have in the home.

- A burner or heat source – A modern stove top heat will be sufficient.
- A tank to hold the main crop.
- A condenser.
- A separator.
- Glass bottles (to store the oils you have extracted)
- Flasks

Before going out and buying what you think will work, it's worthwhile doing a quick research on the Internet, since there are distillery kits for essential oils and some of these are less cumbersome than others and can simply be put away in the kitchen cabinets when not in use. They don't have to look like a witches brewing kit. Compact kits are available for home use and these are not too costly.

A couple of examples can be found here and these seem very comprehensive and meet the requirements you need for producing the oils yourself. Other, more traditional kits can be found even on general websites such as Amazon, though do read the instructions carefully as many of these are glass based. Be aware if you are making your oils in the home that children need to be kept away from heated equipment.

Once you have set the apparatus up you now need to choose the right raw material to extract oil. You can choose any plant materials you want but ideally you should choose dried leaves, flowers, buds, seeds etc. These could have been collected in season and dried ready for the process by using natural drying methods.

Method for distillation of essential oil:

- Fill your holding tank with enough water and slowly put in the plant matter that you have chosen as your base.

- Shut the lid of the tank and place it over the burner and heat it. The temperature should be at least boiling temperature - 100 degree Celsius.

- The water will start bubbling soon and you will notice vapors passing through the condenser. These vapors will eventually cool down to form the oil.

- The condensed vapors or oils will then reach the separator.

- Once you have collected enough oil, turn off the heat and filter the oil through a muslin cloth or cheesecloth. Be sure to filter it properly so that no residue is left. This is relatively straightforward and you can keep a batch of cloth specifically for that purpose.

- Using a clean flask, pour this oil in bottles and shut them tightly. Store these bottles in cool and dark places and away from sunlight to avoid any adverse reaction.

The oils formed by this method are not carrier oils and hence are very volatile and concentrated. Ideally, you should not use these oils without mixing them with carrier oils. The above simple method is used for extracting oils at home but there are other methods as well which are listed below.

Some of the most common ones are as follows:

Solvent extraction

This system is complex and is used on flora which is perhaps too delicate to go through the distillation process. The problem with this kind of extraction is that what you are left with is not particularly pure but is considered as an "absolute." This kind of extraction is used on flowers which are delicate such as gardenia and jasmine, but the oils which are extracted are more used for cosmetic use, rather than therapeutic use which calls for a much stronger oil. In fact, if using the oils for health purposes, absolutes are not as strong as oils which have been distilled and experts are of the opinion that absolutes should not be used by people who are looking for treatment of the immune system, since there is the possibility of residue in the form of pesticides.

Expression

This is a method which is fairly easy to do at home, and involves the rinds of citrus fruits. Centrifugal force is used in this process and spikes will enter the rind allowing the oils to be released during the spinning process. Although this method is popular, the equipment may be expensive. In olden days, the same process was done with sponges and the rind of the fruit was flattened to open up the pores and the sponge used to gather the oils. This was then squeezed from the sponge into a container to collect the oils. You may have heard of this system as it is also called cold pressing and is a common method of extraction.

Distillation

The distillation system used to extract oil is explained at the beginning of this chapter, where details are given as to the equipment used and the process that can be employed at home.

Enfleurage

The Eden Project, which is a nature based project in Cornwall, England, is encouraging visitors to learn the art of enfleurage. As you can see from reading their pages, this is in effect a way to capture the essence of the floral aromas in oil format. Full instructions with images are found on their website and these may be of interest to those concerned with delicate flowers.

Micro-distillation

There is probably no better way to describe this than to present readers with a <u>video</u> of the process which shows the plants being distilled and which gives details of how the process works. The explanation is very full and as you can see, the equipment used is in standard chemistry kit format.

Maceration

Maceration may sound like an easy extraction process but it is far from it and generally only used for large quantities. Similar to solvent based extraction, hot oil is used to extract the aromas from the plants. This may be a little too complex to perform at home.

Phytosol extraction

This method is also complex and uses solvents to extract the oils.

Of all the processes mentioned above, distillation is the most frequently used method for extracting oil. Other than the distillation method shared with you above, there exist other distillation methods, which can be used to extract oils from the plant sources.

There is an <u>overview</u> for those interested in taking up extraction of oil in any quantity, which has been provided by agricultural sources and which may be of interest to those who intend to produce a lot of essential oils.

Let us take a look at the different methods.

Hydro distillation

The method which we used earlier is hydro distillation. In this method the plant material is added to the water to form an isotropic mixture, which releases oil. This oil then gets condensed in the condenser and is then moved to the separator. Oil thus separated can be stored for future use. Ideally the temperature is supposed to be 100 degrees Celsius but it may be changed considering the hardness of the material used. This is one of the oldest as well as one of the most popular methods of extracting essential oils and is the most likely to be used in the home environment.

Steam distillation

This is another form of the distillation method which we looked at above. In this method, the plant material is placed on a screen and steam is passed through it. The temperature is adjusted according to the material and its hardness but it is high enough so as to extract oil.

The essential oils get infused with the constant force of steam and this infused mixture then passes through a condenser thus condensing oil. This condensed mixture is then passed through the separator and the oil is collected. Although this method is quite cheap and easy as well, it requires a large quantity of plant materials to get enough oil, which is why this method is not used quite often and isn't as popular as normal distillation.

Solvent extraction

For this method you will need a hydrocarbon solvent. The oil extracted gets mixed and is filtered and then distilled. You need to use alcohol for this method of extraction. It should be noted that this method does not always yield pure results.

Maceration

This method is one of the most impure methods of extracting essential oils. The raw product is directly placed in carrier oil and then is heated. The secretions of the product get mixed with the oil and this oil is then strained and is ready for use. Because of the impurity of the oil produced and the complexity of the system of extraction, it's unlikely that you would use this method at home.

Enfluerage

This is another ancient practice mainly used to extract perfumes from flowers to make fragrances and perfumes. In a special wooden frame box the flowers are layered with fat. This fat absorbs the essential oils from flower. Finally when enough oil is extracted it is separated from the fat.

The video linked to above shows this being used in a horticultural setting at the Eden Project. People travel from all over the world to see this project which grows plants in domes and which has a wonderful variety of plants available for making essential oils. The old craft of producing these oils is demonstrated to visitors who can take that knowledge home and learn to make their own essential oils.

As you can see from this chapter, the ways in which the oils are extracted are many and the diversity of these methods really depends upon the delicacy of the natural flower being used as some are too delicate to go through the distilling process without losing some of their oils. However, those that use solvents are not the purest forms of oil. Thus, it's a case of swings and roundabouts as to whether you want pure oil or whether you want a quantity of impure oils. Most home producers will opt for the latter option because the results are more consistent and less interference with nature is involved.

Chapter 6:

Useful Essential Oils

Under the next chapter, you will find a variety of recipes of concoctions and mixtures or essential oils, which you can use for treating, preventing and curing many kinds of diseases, disorders etc. All of these recipes or methods are quite easy to follow and anyone can prepare them in a jiffy. But before giving you the recipes, it's worthwhile checking out some of the essential oils and their recognized uses. These are long established uses and thus, even if you only have a small amount of knowledge, you will be able to glean which mixtures are more likely to help you with which illnesses or treatments.

Chamomile Essential Oil

Chamomile oil is a calming oil frequently used to treat nervous symptoms and insomnia. It is also used for anger management and is frequently used in teas. If you are unfamiliar with this, it's a great choice if you are stressed or if you have worries. Chamomile has always been used to help those who are of a nervous disposition and has a calming effect which is helpful to catch up on lost sleep. Remember, sleep serves an extremely important part in good health. Although stressed people tend to sleep less, what they are in fact doing is depriving their bodies of essential time to cure naturally. This is part of good quality sleep and chamomile will help to calm the nerves and give you a good night's sleep.

Neroli Essential Oil

You may be unfamiliar with this name, but Neroli oil is a form of citrus oil. Like many other citrus essential oils it is well known for its relaxing properties. It relieves anxiety. It is also used as an anti-depressant. Neroli also used helps to maintain the balance of hormones in the endocrine system.

Rose Essential Oil

Rose oil is quite famous. It is extracted from rose flowers and it is highly fragrant. It is highly stimulating and boosts the brain power. It activates the mind and increase activity. It is often used with a variety of oils, carriers and other essential oils. It is also used in perfumes.

Angelica essential oil

Angelica is a plant, whose seed, root and fruit are generally used for medical purposes. It has a variety of benefits, ranging from its anti-spasmodic, to diuretic, expectorant, tonic, stimulant, and diaphoretic, digestive, hepatic and nervine properties, among others. Angelica is great for improving one's health. It is especially beneficial for the liver, and helps in toning up the body. Aside from that, angelica can be used to improve digestion, increase urination, flush out toxins, purify the blood, reduce gases, and remove menstrual obstructions. Another benefit of angelica is that it can also be used to remedy nervous disorders.

When combined with other herbs, angelica may be effective in treating premature ejaculation as well.

Bitter almond essential oil

This one has a very interesting use- it cures hydrophobia! Bitter almond essential oil is commonly used for a wide range of purposes, like other essential oils. It can be used as a bactericide, vermifuge, fungicide, anesthetic, sedative, anti-intoxicant and aperients. Bitter almond essential oil is quite effective in eradicating worms, killing fungi, bacteria and germs. Bitter almond essential oil cleanses the body, as it successfully flushes out excess salt, toxins and water from the body.

Black Pepper essential oil

The unripe, red fruit of the Piper nigrum plant are used for the extraction of black pepper oil. The oil is spicy and induces warmth in the body, thus proving excellent as a remedy for colds. It is highly beneficial for curing sore muscles and joint aches too. Black pepper essential oil aids circulation and bruising and helps with rheumatoid arthritis. The most common uses of black pepper oil include the treatment of muscular aches, nerve tonic and fevers, pain relief, stimulation of appetite, enabling of peristalsis, facilitating proper digestion.

Overuse of black pepper essential oil may cause irritation of the skin, or over-stimulation of the kidneys. Overall, the therapeutic properties of black pepper essential oil are digestive, diuretic, laxative, anti-spasmodic, analgesic and antiseptic in nature.

Camphor essential oil

This oil is extracted from the Cinnamomum Camphora plant. While the oil has a few toxic properties, it is very valuable when it comes to remedying colds. It can be used as a part of vapor therapy to clear the lungs, calm nervous depression and dispel apathy. It may be used in your daily beauty regime, as camphor oil has a variety of distinct skin benefits. The therapeutic properties of camphor essential oil are of antiseptic, diuretic, febrifuge, cardiac, analgesic, antidepressant, and stimulant, sudorific and vulnerary in nature, among others.

What this entails, is that camphor oil is great as a component of treatment of acne, inflammation, muscular aches, rheumatism, colds, fevers, nervous depression, flu and other infectious diseases. Unlike the majority of other essential oils, camphor should be avoided at all costs when it comes to aromatherapy, owing to its toxic properties. It is best used in vapor therapy, and sometimes even in compresses.

Cinnamon Essential Oil

Extracted from the Cinnamomum zylanicum plant, cinnamon essential oil is spicy and is very beneficial in aromatherapy. The oil has a warm, musky, spicy fragrance, and the colour of the oil varies from yellow when extracted from the leaf, to red-brown when extracted from the bark. In aromatherapy, cinnamon leaf oil is generally used.

The therapeutic properties of cinnamon include, but are not restricted to antiseptic, analgesic, cardiac, aphrodisiac, antibiotic, tonic, stimulant and vermifuge. This oil is effective for driving away colds and flu, and reducing depression and weakness. It acts as a great reliever of exhaustion, and is of great use to ease menstrual pains. As for its antibiotic properties, cinnamon essential oil can be used for the treatment of infected respiratory tracts. It also helps with rheumatism, general pains and arthritis.

Frankincense Essential Oil

Extracted from resin of the Boswellia carteri tree, frankincense essential oil is one of the most popular choices when it comes to aromatherapy. This oil has a cooling impact on the brain and serves to make internal peace, while soothing the respiratory and urinary tract, and pain related to stiffness and muscular aches. The oil has a reviving and invigorating effect of the skin.

The therapeutic properties of frankincense oil are germicide, astringent, and carminative, cicatrisant, cytophylactic, digestive, expectorant, calming, tonic, uterine, vulnerary and expectorant.

The oil helps in calming the psyche, helping with respiration and is fantastic for meditation purposes. Also, it helps with depression and suppressing anxiety problems. When it comes to the respiratory tract, frankincense is useful as it clears the lungs and assists with shortness of breath, asthma, bronchitis, laryngitis, hacks and colds. It is beneficial for women and their menstrual problems as it helps in overcoming menstrual pains, and acts as a tonic for the uterus and is helpful during labor.

Great for wounds, frankincense essential oil acts as a skin tonic and is effective on bruises, wounds, scars and sores.

Jasmine Essential Oil

Jasmine essential oil is extricated from Jasminum Gradiflora plant of the Oleaceae family. Albeit expensive, this oil accomplishes more than being exotic smelling - it unwinds and lifts depression and enables confidence, eases labor, assists with sexual problems, soothes cough and tones and enhances skin elasticity, while serving to lessen stretch marks and scars.

The helpful properties of jasmine oil are anti-depressant, sedative, antiseptic, cicatrisant, expectorant, galactagogue, parturient, calming and uterine, among others. Jasmine oil is effective for depression, helping calm the nerves and reinstating a feeling of contentment, happiness and confidence, while revitalizing the body. It encourages healthy labor, by fortifying contractions and relieving pain. It is great for use during post-natal depression and also facilitates the flow of breast milk. Due to its profoundly calming nature, jasmine oil assists with sexual issues, such as premature ejaculation, impotency and frigidity.

When it comes to the respiratory tract, again, jasmine is really helpful. It relieves bothersome cough and helps with laryngitis. Aside from that, it also helps with sore muscles, sprains and stiff joints. For the skin, jasmine has a cooling effect. As mentioned earlier, it assists elasticity. Also, jasmine oil helps tone delicate, greasy and dry skin, and is effective in reducing scarring.

Pine Essential Oil

Extracted from the Pinus sylvestris tree of the Pinaceae family, pine essential oil has many therapeutic properties, including, but not limited to antimicrobial, antiseptic, antiviral, bactericidal, , deodorant, diuretic, expectorant, hypertensive, insecticidal, restorative, as well as stimulant, among others.

Most beneficial in providing relief from fatigue, pine essential oil can be used in vapor therapy to provide one with an invigorating effect. Mental, sexual and physical fatigue is effectively treated with pine essential oil. Aside from fatigue, pine essential oil can be used to treat cuts and sores. Its warming properties are of great use in treating rheumatism, muscular aches and pains, and it can be used to help with asthma, laryngitis, colds and flu as well. Lice and scabies may be gotten rid of too by using pine essential oil. Not only this, it also acts as a cleanser for the kidneys, and prevents urinary infections.

Nutmeg Essential Oil

This spicy and warming essential oil is commonly used to fight inflammation and muscle pain through aromatherapy. Nutmeg essential oil has a stimulating and invigorating effect on the mind as well. The nature of the therapeutic properties of nutmeg essential oil range from analgesic to , anti-rheumatic, laxative, antiseptic, digestive, antispasmodic, carminative, stimulant and tonic.

Nutmeg essential oil is effective in stimulating the heart and aids circulation, making the mind more active. It is great for people who suffer from fainting spells. The digestive tract is strengthened as a result of the usage of nutmeg essential oil. It has other benefits too, such as relief from nausea, diarrhea, and chronic vomiting.

Nutmeg induces a healthy appetite and helps in avoiding constipation, and also acts as a tonic for the reproductive system, fighting impotence, frigidity and scanty periods. Nutmeg also provides much needed relief from muscle pains.

Tea Tree Essential Oil

One of the most important and potent of all essential oils, tea tree essential oil has a light spicy fragrance, and is extracted from Melaleuca alternifolia. It is very effective in ensuring the proper health of one's immune system. The use of tea tree oil is becoming predominant in the cosmetic industry for its many benefits. Tea tree oil successfully helps in increasing the body's immunity and warding off diseases and infections.

Tea tree essential oil can help with cold sores, glandular fever, influenza, asthma, whooping cough, sinusitis, tuberculosis and bronchial congestion. When it comes to the genital –urinary system, tea tree oil is beneficial in treating cystitis, vaginal thrush and warts, among other genital infections. Tea tree essential oil has anti-inflammatory properties and helps with acne, burns, greasy skin, herpes, infected wounds, blemishes and sunburns.

Rosemary Essential Oil

This is likely to be an oil that is made from plants in the garden and is very useful for digestive problems. Used also to help with muscle strain, the oil gives off an aroma which is useful as an anti-inflammatory and can be applied either in a topical cream, which would be bought rather than home produced, or in a massage treatment.

Sandalwood Essential Oil

Sandalwood oil is very commonly used oil in the Indian subcontinent. Sandalwood oil is extracted from the wood of the sandalwood tree. It is quite costly and is considered holy in India. It is predominantly used in India and is closely related to Yoga and related schools of health. It is highly relaxing and helps in calming the mind. It is also used to maintain a proper balance of emotions. Thus, this is an ideal essential oil if you are practicing meditation and wish to create an atmosphere of calm.

Thyme Essential Oil

This is another garden based plant which can be used for oil extraction. The benefits of thyme are well known to help ward off the effects of winter or changing of seasons, as it helps to cleanse the skin, helping it to ward off those seasonal changes. Thyme is useful for strengthening the nerves, and helps with concentration and memory. Thyme helps relieve exhaustion and fatigue, and fights depression. When it comes to common ailments, thyme is rather effective in treating whooping coughs, colds, flu, sinusitis, asthma, laryngitis, and sore throats. Thyme boosts the immune system and acts as a urinary antiseptic.

Thyme has a warming effect that can help with poor circulation and help with sprains and ports injuries. Thyme also effective when it comes to anorexia, scanty periods, cellulite and obesity.

Clove Essential Oil

It's quite likely that you are already aware of this little beauty. In the health of gums and teeth, it's vital but cloves are more valuable than that and also help heart health and act as an antioxidant.

Basil Essential Oil

You can probably see a pattern here as many of the plants mentioned are those which are easily grown in the herb garden. Basil is no exception. This is used to help calm problems with sore muscles. Thus, a perfect time to use it would be after a sports event or session. It also has the ability to treat breathing problems and to help the skin to stay cool in the summer months.

Eucalyptus Essential Oil

If you have ever eaten cough sweets or pastilles, then you may have noticed that this is a common flavor. Eucalyptus oil is said to be a natural coolant. It has a cooling and deodorizing effect on the body, and helps in treating fevers, malaria and migraine. For the respiratory tract, it is effective for treating coughs, asthma, throat infections, and sinusitis. It also has anti-inflammatory properties, soothing inflammation and easing mucus, eliminating stuffiness due to colds and hay fever.

It may be used as a warming oil when suffering from muscular pains, sprains or poor circulation. Eucalyptus essential oil is quite effective for burns, cuts, wounds, blisters and other skin conditions. When down with measles, chicken pox or flue, one can use eucalyptus oil to achieve some relief.

Fennel Essential Oil

This is a very typical lady's treatment as it deals with painful menstrual problems. It also works on the lymphatic system and keeps it in healthy check. Fennel is primarily a remedy for digestion related problems, such as constipation, flatulence, anorexia, nausea, vomiting and hiccups. It may be used to treat obesity, since it promotes the feeling of being full and has a diuretic effect which disperses cellulite.

Fennel is good for mental health too, promoting a feeling of strength and courage. On the skin, it has a cleansing and toning effect, proving effective in treating bruises, fighting wrinkles and reducing greasiness. Aside from the skin, it has a soothing and toning effect on the spleen and liver as well.

Lavender Essential Oil

Everyone loves the smell of lavender for good reason. It's a feel good aroma which helps to calm the mind, but it does more than that. It's great for skin irritations and for easing of headaches caused by bad posture or stressful pains in the shoulders and neck. Thus, in this day and age, it is very popular in use.

Wild Orange Essential Oil

That zesty aroma of orange helps so many things. When your mom encouraged you to eat oranges for vitamin C, she wasn't kidding. The oils from the wild orange help to ward off colds but they also help you to protect yourself from environmental changes, help the immune system to stay alert and help to energize.

Peppermint Essential Oil

This is a typical favorite for breathing problems but it is also used to help the digestive system. This is an absolute must for the family and will help considerably with day to day living.

These are some of the frequently used and popular oils which can be used by mixing with carrier oils to make blends which can serve multiple purposes. These can also be vaporized if wanting to create a super atmosphere and can be used for bathing or for topical use, depending upon the purpose of the treatment. Please remember not to use neat essential oils. The carrier makes the oils go further but it also stops any potential sting.

Chapter 7:

Ailments that can be Cured with the Help of Essential Oils

Frostbite

When affected with frostbite, the skin becomes numb and pale due to insufficient and poor circulation, on long exposure to cold temperature. The first areas to be affected are generally the fingers and toes, as well as the ears. Some parts of the face are also prone to frostbite, such as the chin and the nose. Warming up the affected area to restore circulation and cure the frostbite may sometimes cause pain and irritation, and lead to some swelling. Frostbite results in damage of blood vessels and tissues due to lack of circulation.

Using essential oils such as pine and cypress in a massage can resolve circulation problems. These essential oils should not be used directly, and must instead be diluted in carrier oil. If you have been out in the snow the entire day, you can use a little grape seed oil, combined with a few drops of pine oil, and massage your feet with it. Yet another essential oil that can be used for massage, to relieve frostbite is neat lavender oil. Apply it to patches of affected skin for relief.

High Blood pressure

One of the most important things for a person suffering from hypertension to do is monitor their blood pressure on a daily basis. This is done as a precautionary measure, to avoid health problems such as angina, strokes, arteriosclerosis and thrombosis. High blood pressure is a common cardiovascular concern among people these days, and needs to be treated and contained to prevent it from getting very serious.

Oils that can help with high blood pressure include marjoram, lavender, lemon, ylang ylang, and clary sage. Along with a carrier oil, essential oils applied topically on a regular basis can help a great deal with regulating blood pressure. Gentle massage with these oils can prove to be very relaxing.

However, some oils are to be avoided by patients suffering from hypertension. These are sage, thyme, rosemary and hyssop, as they contain compounds that may elevate blood pressure.

Boils

Boils can be defined as an outgrowth; an abscess generally located at the hairline, underarms or the buttocks. A few ailments, such as fatigue, fever, and lymph glands may also be associated with boils. Boils occur predominantly in young males as a result of a diet reliant on fried foods which lead to blood impurities.

Lavender, juniper, tea tree oil and chamomile oil have been proven useful in the treatment of boils. If used in a combination with hot water and applied on the area, the boil may subside soon.

Constipation

Constipation, as you must know, is the condition where a person experiences difficulty in passing stools, or the absence of an urge to do so. Constipation is indication by a loss in appetite, mild nausea and indigestion. Pre-menstrual and pregnant women are known to suffer from constipation at times. The most common cause of indigestion or constipation is the lack of fiber and roughage in one's diet.

To help with constipation, essential oils such as lemon oil, peppermint oil, jojoba oil and rosemary oil may be used. A combination of these oils used to massage the lower abdomen two to three times a day can lead to much relief.

Bleeding Gums

Bleeding gums are the result of an infection or inflammation of the gums, also known as gingivitis. The cause of bleeding gums is often irritation due to the plaque residing in the mouth. If the plaque in the mouth is allowed to harden and accumulate, it may lead to a severe condition called periodontis. So, it is imperative that you take care of bleeding gums the moment they appear. Inflamed gums can be held responsible for more dental problems and loss of teeth than tooth decay.

Essential oils have the cure to this problem as well. A mouthwash made from thyme oil, chamomile oil, peppermint oil, eucalyptus oil, some brandy and water can help a great deal with reducing bleeding of gums.

Cough

Cough is the response of the body to irritation caused in the respiratory tract, whether it be in the lungs, throat or the bronchial tubes. While coughing helps expel mucus and other irritating substances from the body, they can cause much discomfort. Coughs are generally accompanied by a cold or a viral or bacterial infection of any other kind, such as pneumonia. Cigarette smoke and pollution are also contributors to cough.

Essential oils may be used in mixtures you may leave beside your bed, or mixtures that you can consume to help with coughs. Essential oils that are most beneficial for this purpose are eucalyptus, lemon, thyme, pine and jojoba. Massage oils made with a combination of the aforementioned oils can also provide great relief.

Cold and Flu

Runny nose, sneezing, sore throats and dry coughs are the most common indicators of a cold or flu. Due to this, the lymph glands in the neck may become swollen and sensitive. The extent to which colds affect people varies from each person to the next. Flu is generally much more serious than a cold, but it exhibits similar symptoms. Along with the symptoms of a cold, flu is accompanied by chills and high fever, and a feeling of utter exhaustion and inability to muster energy to do any work. The muscles become sore and ache, providing much discomfort.

Home remedies involving essential oils are a really effective way to get rid of a flu or cold. Essential oils that assist the eradication of colds and flu are clove oil, pine oil, eucalyptus oil, cinnamon oil, Niaouli oil. When combined with hot water and used as a spray, these oils prove to be quite beneficial. Another oil that may relieve the stuffiness experienced during colds is cajuput, when combines with the others and used in an inhaler or a massage oil.

Earache

Middle-ear infections are generally the cause for earache. You might have experienced this at some point, and know that it can be highly infuriating. Shooting pains in ears, vomiting, a feeling of noises and fullness in the ears are common symptoms of an ear infection. While experiencing an ear infection, the first and foremost concern is to get rid of the shooting pains.

For relief from the pain, clove essential and grape seed oil used together as a massage oil can help a great deal. If the ear infection is a result of a throat infection, then tea tree oil might be a more suitable choice.

Heartburn

Characterized by a burning pain that occurs in the chest, heartburn may sometimes radiate upwards to the neck, throat and even face. Generally, heartburn occurs after a meal, when the acids present in the stomach reflux past the sphincter. If the muscle tone is lost, it leads to the pain of heartburn.

As with most ailments, there is a remedy for this condition too by the use of essential oils. Massaging the upper abdominal area with a mixture of fennel essential oil, peppermint oil, eucalyptus oil and grape seed oil can provide relief.

Insomnia

The inability or the delay in falling asleep is known as insomnia. Insomnia is most commonly the result of excessive stress or anxiety, as well as physical conditions such as PMS or menopause, in women. An unhealthy lifestyle that incorporates smoking with an imbalanced diet, with little to zero exercise can be a major contributor to insomnia.

To cure insomnia, it is important to get the body to a state of relaxation. This can be achieved with the use of essential oils such as lavender, clary sage, Petitgrain, ylang ylang and neroli. You may use them in your bath or as massage oils.

Nausea

Nausea, unlike the ailments mentioned before is a result of both physiological and psychological distress. Triggers for nausea include bad digestion, flu, migraine, repulsive smells and food poisoning, along with motion sickness and early pregnancy.

Vapor therapy is the most effective way of using essential oils as a remedy for nausea. Fresh and soothing essential oils such as lavender and bergamot can make one feel much better. These oils may simply be used on a handkerchief for sniffing while overcome with a feeling of a discomfort. You should experience relief soon.

Sore throat

Pharyngitis, more commonly known as sore throat is a result of inflammation of the pharynx. The common types of sore throat include tonsillitis, or an infection which is viral or bacterial in nature. This is generally accompanied by a runny nose, muscle pain and fever. Sore throats can be very painful in nature, and are difficult to get rid of.

However, with the use of essential oils, the recovery can be sped up. A massage oil applied on the neck, the back and the ears can provide relief to someone suffering from a sore throat. The essential oils that are the most useful for treating a sore throat are thyme, lemon, and chamomile and tea tree oil. Essential oils may also be added to a steam machine. Steam inhalation is a great way of relieving one of a sore throat.

Wounds

Wounds must always be sterilized to prevent further infection from affecting the area and settling in. To prevent this, a bath may be prepared for the area using essential oils such as lavender and tea tree oil. They have been known to be very effective.

Chapter 8:

Suggested Recipes for Various Ailments

Since many of the essential oils have overlapping properties to help with ailments, they can be mixed and the recipes below will be useful for you to try. Some are common sense recipes using two oils that serve the same purpose but give a varied aroma when mixed. Others may not be so obvious but you might like to try them and see if they help with health associated problems which may be common in your family.

It should always be remembered that a carrier must be used if these oils are to come in contact with the skin. The amount of oil as opposed to carrier should be in the quantities shown here:

For Topical Use

If you are using a pure form or Therapeutic Grade Essential oil you can apply directly to the skin or if using on sensitive skin or small children, mix with a carrier oil like coconut oil or olive oil.

For Bathing

Use 6 – 8 drops of oil. Milk can be used as a substitute for carrier oil.

Inhalation

3-4 drops can be used in boiling water to be breathed in under a towel. However, if you use a diffuser or vaporizer, then you can use 9-10 drops depending upon the strength of odor you wish to produce.

Although you will find this information elsewhere in the book, we thought it important that this should be shown in the recipe section to remind you not to overdo it. Essential oils are very strong and if you use them wisely, a little can go a very long way.

Be very aware of your mixtures and it's a good idea to label them. Labels will give you an instant overview of the oils that you have and you can actually buy labels commercially or simply use self-adhesive labels that you have written the blend onto. There are many free printable on the Internet and if you go into Google Images and type in a search for Essential Oil Label Printables, you will find there are many to suit your particular liking.

Bottles

It may be a sensible idea to buy vials which have a dropper. This helps you to make your essential oils go further and to be more accurate when you are mixing recipes. If you don't use a dropper, you tend to get too many drops as the liquid flows too quickly. Pharmacies are the best place to get these, although of course, there will be online sources for vials with a dropper attachment.

Why colored glass?

Essential oils need the protection of colored glass because it makes them last longer and keep all of their natural properties intact. Don't be tempted to use clear glass as your oils will lose their aroma or may even evaporate.

Lemon, Lavender and Clary Sage Mixture

This particular mixture is very relevant to today's lifestyle. It may be useful for the bath for relaxing. It may also be very helpful in a home office environment, as it promotes anti stress properties that help you to relax.

Ingredients:

- 8 drops Clary sage essential oil
- 2-4 drops Lavender essential oil
- 2-4 drops Lemon essential oil

Procedure

1. Take a small and dark glass container and add the quoted number of drops of essential oils into it.
2. Shake the container and then roll it slowly in your palms to mix the oils well.

Stress Buster Recipe

Since both of these oils are stress busters, this is the ideal mix for people who want to create a calming atmosphere. This mixture is very suitable for using in a vaporizer in the bedroom area. It can help people who are recovering from illness or help those who are stressed.

Ingredients:

- 2-4 drops Lavender essential oil
- 1 drop Vetiver essential oil

Procedure:

1. Take a small and dark glass vial; clean and dry it thoroughly.
2. Add all the ingredients one by one into the vial.
3. Roll the vial in between your palms to mix the oils properly.

Liver Health Essential Blend

This is a recipe which is great for liver health. It is also very good for stress and for clear skin. Thus, it can be used either topically or in a vaporizer. The added Frankincense oil is worth it because this oil is used to promote and build up healthy immune system reactions, help cellular health and believe it or not, it can help you to get rid of scars such as stretch marks.

Ingredients:

- 2-4 drops Bergamot essential oil
- 2-4 drops Geranium essential oil
- 2-4 drops Frankincense essential oil

Procedure:

1. Take a small and dark glass vial and clean and dry it thoroughly.
2. Add all the ingredients one by one in the vial, first the bergamot oil, then germanium and lastly the frankincense.
3. Roll the vial in between your palms to mix the oils properly.
4. This recipe can be used in a vaporizer for those suffering from liver problems or who want to benefit from relaxation properties. However, if used for stretch marks, it needs to be applied together with a carrier oil to the area of skin in question.

Grapefruit Detox Mixture

This is a recipe which is great for detoxing the skin but also as a detox in general because the mixture was chosen to combine the detox properties of citrus fruit with the subtlety of perfume provided by Jasmine. You can actually use the grapefruit with any floral oil to give a great recipe for detoxing. If used for menstrual cramps, the Clary Sage really sets of the recipe to perfection.

Ingredients:

- 6 drops Grapefruit essential oil
- 2 drops Clary Sage essential oil
- 2 drops Jasmine essential oil

Procedure:

1. Take a small and dark glass vial and clean and dry it thoroughly.
2. Add all the ingredients one by one in the vial, first Clary Sage then Jasmine and lastly Grapefruit.
3. Roll the vial in between your palms to mix the oils properly.
4. The recipe above is a good one for those who suffer greatly from menstrual problems and who are looking for instant boost and relief from pain.

Better Skin Blend

The oils chosen for this complex recipe deal with skin problems, mental wellbeing, menstrual cramps and detoxing all at the same time. Suitable for people who are finding life stressful, this recipe carries a hefty weight in helping you to recover quickly from all of the stresses that life throws at you. If this is being prepared for a male, then the ylang ylang content is not so vital.

Ingredients:

- 1-2 drops Grapefruit essential oil
- 2- 4 drops Bergamot essential oil
- 4 drops Blood Orange essential oil
- 2-4 drops Ylang Ylang essential oil
- 2-4 drops Patchouli essential oil

Procedure:

1. Take a small and dark glass vial and clean and dry it thoroughly.
2. Add bergamot oil and blood orange oil. Shake. Now add the rest of the ingredients.
3. Roll the vial in between your palms to mix the oils properly.
4. The recipe shown above is used for many different ailments. However, if mixed with a carrier cream, it can be applied to the forehead to relieve stress and to help create calm.

Headache Mixture

This mixture is known to be beneficial for headaches and thus has been singled out for this purpose, since headaches are common in this day and age and the mixture is likely to be used on a regular basis to stave off those tension headaches.

Ingredients:

- 7 drops Basil
- 7 drops Rosemary oil
- 80 ml sweet Almond oil
- 14 drops Lavender oil

Procedure:

1. Take a small and dark glass vial and clean and dry it thoroughly.
2. Add all the ingredients one by one in the vial.
3. Roll the vial in between your palms to mix the oils properly.
4. Inhale the oil for an instant stress relieving effect. You can use it as a balm as well, though in the case of a balm, mix the oil with an equal proportion of carrier oil.

Lemon Fragrance Balm

If you want to mix your own balms, then bees wax acts as a carrier and only a small quantity of oils is required to go a very long way. This particular balm recipe is to give the skin a real tonic. It helps to cleanse the skin of environmental impurities and to keep the skin in tip top condition.

Ingredients:

- 3 tablespoons Bees Wax
- 3 tablespoons Jujube Oil
- 30 drops Lemon Oil

Procedure:

1. Take a double boiler and melt the beeswax.
2. Once melted add the Jujube oil slowly in it.
3. Remove from heat.
4. Slowly add the lemon oil in this mixture. Pour this in a vial.
5. Balms can also be placed into a container, provided that the container is sufficiently protective. Small tins are often used for balms and these are suitable to carry in your handbag.

Lift Your Spirits

There is nothing quite like a sweet aroma to brighten up your day. The ingredients of this recipe have been chosen because of their ability to lift your spirit and help to relieve tension and stress. This recipe is particularly good to carry with you if you are going out in hot weather and you want the calming effect of the oils to help you to keep your cool.

Ingredients:

- 3 drops of Peppermint
- 2 drops of Wild Orange

Procedure:

1. Apply the Wild Orange to feet and wrists and layer with 2 drops of Peppermint.
2. Add on Drop of Peppermint to the back of your neck for cooling.

Sweet Melody

This is a choice recipe for a winter's day because the combined aromas are extremely good for stress relief but also have a touch of winter aroma mixed with the healing power of geranium. Woody oils are great for detoxing and the floral scent added by geranium and lavender add a wonderfully scented addition that helps to relieve stress and give out a feel good factor.

Ingredients:

- 3 drops Lavender oil
- 4 drops Cedar wood oil
- 3 drops Geranium oil

Procedure:

1. Take a small and dark glass vial and clean and dry it thoroughly.
2. Add all the ingredients one by one in the vial.
3. Roll the vial in between your palms to mix the oils properly.

Cedar wood and Lemon Mixture

Known for its detoxing properties, the choice of oils used here also accounts for changes in weather and stuffed up noses. The refreshing aroma of lemon mixes well with the cedar wood and the overall effect of the mix is that it is therapeutic for colds and flu and also for a general feeling of well-being. This is a winter night mix but can equally be used for a cold morning or evening.

Ingredients:

- 1-2 drops Lemon
- 1-2 drops Cedar Wood
- 2-4 drops Lavender

Procedure:

1. Take a small and dark glass vial and make sure that it is clean and dry.
2. Mix the oils into the vial.
3. Place the cap on the vial and roll this between the palms of your hands to ensure that the oils are completely mixed together.
4. This blend makes for a great balm as well and in the case of a balm you would need to mix the blend with bees wax as explained in an earlier recipe using the same amount of ingredients and placing the balm into a container that is easily carried around.

Digestive Soothing Blend

Yet another ideal winter blend, this blend can also be used for digestive problems. Ginger is well known to help with digestion. Marjoram on the other hand supports the cardio vascular system and also the immune system. Thus, if you use this as a general vaporization mix, you will find that the room in which it is used is extremely atmospheric and will help you to overcome problems.

Ingredients:

- 1-2 drops marjoram essential oil
- 2-4 drops ginger essential oil
- 2-4 drops rosewood essential oil

Procedure:

1. Take a small and dark glass vial and clean and dry it thoroughly
2. Add all the ingredients one by one in the vial.
3. Roll the vial in between your palms to mix the oils properly.

Immune Support Blend

Looking at the ingredients of this recipe, you will see that this is the perfect mix for protecting the immune system. Frankincense is known for its healing properties and the woody aromas added to it help mental well-being.

Ingredients:

- 4 drops frankincense essential oil
- 2-4 drops rosewood essential oil

Procedure:

1. Take a small and dark glass vial and clean and dry it thoroughly
2. Add all the ingredients one by one in the vial first balsam oil, then frankincense and lastly rosewood.
3. Roll the vial in between your palms to mix the oils properly.
4. The best use of this recipe is certainly to place it into a vaporizer and to allow the aroma to fill the room. It's a heady aroma but it's one which will reap great results, leaving those within the room feeling less stressed and also much healthier.

Refreshing Magic

Consider this recipe as your body's spring clean. The citrus fruits are capable of cleansing the system and will make you feel refreshed. Citrus fruits are great for use during the winter months, but can also waken the body ready for the spring and summer. Think of the recipe as an almost all-the-year-round cleanse, as the detoxification value of the ingredients is well recorded.

Ingredients:

- 20 drops grapefruit essential oil
- 6-8 drops lemon essential oil
- 2 drops Ylang Ylang essential oil
- 1 tablespoon sea salt

Procedure:

1. Take a small and dark glass vial and clean and dry it thoroughly
2. Mix all the ingredients together.
3. Roll the vial in between your palms to mix the oils properly.
4. Inhale frequently.
5. In fact, you will find this mixture so effective that it's likely that you will keep a mixture ready for the diffuser or vaporizer to put on at a moment's notice when you feel the need for a detox,

Minty Magic

As mentioned previously, mint is magic when it comes to digestion and breathing. This is a superb mixture for the after dinner period when guests are relaxing but feeling rather over indulged. It's also a great remedy for people who suffer from digestive problems in general since it will ease the digestive process and make users less likely to suffer from acid reflux.

Ingredients:

- 25 drops peppermint oil
- 2-4 drops Spearmint oil
- 2-4 drops ylang ylang essential oil
- 1 tablespoon sea salt

Procedure:

1. Take a small and dark glass vial and clean and dry it thoroughly
2. Add all the ingredients one by one in the vial.
3. Roll the vial in between your palms to mix the oils properly.
4. The benefit of this oil is that you can keep it in a vaporizer in the dining area of your home and the family will become accustomed to the aroma without even being aware that you are helping each one of them with their digestive processes. The pleasant aroma is one that the family will also enjoy.

Organic Oil Mixture

There are several recipes which stand out for their ability to give instant relief. In this case, curb your hunger pains with a great mix of herbal extracts which really does work. It's a great mixture to use in a vaporizer in the kitchen especially if you are trying your best to diet, but failing miserably. It may just curb your appetite sufficiently to stop you from snacking, while giving your kitchen a wonderful aroma of herbs and healthy food which may change your eating habits.

Ingredients:

- 20 drops basil oil
- 20 drops marjoram oil
- 2 drops oregano oil
- 2 drops thyme essential oil
- 1 tablespoon sea salt

Procedure:

1. Take a small and dark glass vial and clean and dry it thoroughly
2. Add all the ingredients one by one in the vial.
3. Roll the vial in between your palms to mix the oils properly.

Sandalwood Oil Mixture

Although it is rare to ingest essential oils, this mixture is a safe mixture for anyone who is adult and is extremely useful for boosting the mental powers and for uplifting the spirit. There are anti-inflammatory properties to this mixture which are useful in the case of muscle problems, water retention, etc., and the natural diuretic qualities of the mixture also help the digestion process, in that it curbs unhealthy snacking or cravings.

Ingredients:

- 1-2 drops sandalwood essential Oil
- 1-2 drops virgin olive oil
- 1 drop honey
- 1/2 glass soy milk – unsweetened

Procedure:

1. Take a small and dark glass vial and clean and dry it thoroughly
2. Add all the ingredients one by one in the vial.
3. Roll the vial in between your palms to mix the mixture properly

Chapter 9:

Enjoying the Benefits of Aromatherapy

Now that you have an overview of the use of essential oils, this book should serve as a reminder on how to use oils correctly and which oils are good for what purposes. There are of course many oils that you will find in the stores or that you may produce yourself. One thing is sure and that is when you start to use them and feel the benefits, you will incorporate them into your lifestyle because of the great feeling of well-being the oils give you and your family.

From a young age, children will benefit from the use of oils which promote great breathing. Since many kids these days suffer from asthma, aromatherapy helps to clear their air passages when used in a vaporizer. Most children will recall the use of rubs when they were children and topical rubs using the eucalyptus and peppermint aromatherapy oils can help with breathing even in children who are merely trying to stave off colds.

These are also useful for the elderly, since they are non invasive treatments that do not have reactions when used with standard medications. They are able to relieve stress, help the immune system to remain active in warding off infections. They help digestion and so many other problems that are faced by people every day of their lives.

Teens who are introduced to natural balms and health treatments derived from essential oils will find that they will suffer less skin problems and thus enjoy their teen years free of the problems associated with skin, at an age when it really matters. Did you also know that essential oils can promote healthy growth of hair? Indeed they can, and this is another area where your teen may want to get up close and personal with nature.

There's an extremely <u>helpful chart </u>which will show you which oils to use for which hair types and this may be useful when deciding upon which essential oils you would like to introduce to your teens or even use yourself to produce shiny hair.

If you have not tried essential oils, then be careful to look out for good quality oils which are pure, for reasons already stated. The results you get will depend upon the quality of the oils purchased. Since even the more expensive oils do not cost that much, it makes sense to buy the best.

You may wonder how aromas can have such a great effect on health. Imagine for a moment and close your eyes while you do this. Think of all the positive aromas that you remember from childhood. Think of a summer's day, think of the aroma of flowers or even compare the feel good factor with the aroma of freshly baked bread or a hot pot of coffee. Aromas work on the senses. The day to day scents that you associate with healing are all available from nature, though manufacturers have made it easy for you to have these in oil format so that you can have the benefit of those aromas you need to promote great health and wellbeing.

The positivity that aromatherapy promotes means that stress can be a thing of the past or that when it happens, you have an instant remedy to perk you up and make you feel at one with the world.

Aromatherapy takes the best of nature and serves it up for you to use as and when you feel the need to be pampered by something other than pharmaceutically produced medicines.

You may not be aware of it, but your use of essential oils can also benefit pets who reside with you. The anti-inflammatory actions of essential oils may just help your pets more than you know, as well as helping you to have healthier cells in your body, better circulation, healthier hair growth and a general sense of calm. Now those are all good reasons to start your experience of aromatherapy and enjoy the benefits of what nature has to offer you, putting aside the products which may be chock full with chemicals which pollute your body.

Your muscles will relax and feel younger. Your general overview on life will become more positive and you leave yourself less open to infection by protecting your body simply by using the aromas of nature. The same use has been given to essential oils for many centuries though these days; the oils are available easily without having to harvest the crops to provide them. However, you also have the choice of whether to buy those essential oils already extracted or to take the full journey into the world of aromatherapy and extract your own oils from the produce of your garden.

Aromatherapy is more established than you may have imagined and by beginning your experience with tried and tested aromas, such as eucalyptus and peppermint, you can gradually build up your confidence and add more oils to your collection as and when health needs require you to. The subject of aromatherapy is a vast one but the experience that you gain through your day to day use of essential oils adds to your database of knowledge and eventually you will be able to choose the right essential oils to fit each set of circumstances or each season, so that your family derives the best possible protection against illness and the best potential relief from the effects of aches and pains that occur at any age.

It's important to follow safety instructions which come with your oils, or which are outlined earlier in this book, to avoid skin irritation or ingestion of oils which are not intended to be ingested. With these safety instructions in mind, remember to keep your aromatherapy essential oils in a safe place away from children. Little hands can be very tempted by pretty small bottles.

Personalize your experience by having your own style of bottles and by labeling all of your mixtures so that they are available for future use. Having a small container where all of your vials can be kept makes perfect sense, as these oils will last a fair amount of time provided they are stored in a cool place within colored bottles.

It's amazing to think that one or two drops of oil can make the difference between depression and positive attitude. It's even more amazing that nature has provided the answer to many of the health problems suffered by human beings. Phytotherapy has used the goodness of plants to treat people with all kinds of disorders, though these treatments are given by qualified practitioners. In the case of essential oils, even those with very little experience can glean the benefits of their use and this book gives sufficient information for you to have the confidence to try.

Conclusion

Here ends the wonderful journey through the mysterious world of aromatic essential oils. These oils are not only sweet smelling but are also extremely useful for physical and mental health. These oils will help you improve your physical health and mental frame of mind.

Essential oils are one of the oldest forms of medicines. They are natural, herbal and effective. The methods of extraction given in this book will definitely help you to extract oil at home with ease especially bearing in mind the modern, convenient tools that are available to the individual. Common sense precautions should be taken while working on extracting the oils, since often the apparatus is of a delicate nature or uses extreme heat. Thus, keeping children away from the area being used is a wise move.

In this book, you will also find that the writer has included wonderful recipes, which you can use for a variety of ailments. These recipes should serve as guidelines to help you to create your own recipes. Feel free to experiment with your oils and mix different oils together to create your own family recipes that suit the needs of your friends and family.

Find out the benefits of your own new mixtures and share the news with friends. People have been doing this for so many centuries that you may even find you are using the same remedy as was used in Roman times. That proves the validity of the studies which were done back then, since the oils being extracted from plants are still recognized as being of great benefit to the health and welfare of users.

Lastly, it is hoped that you found this book interesting and useful and that you will be tempted to try essential oils for yourself. It is hoped that you will use it frequently. I wish you and your family mental peace, spiritual strength and physical health all of which can be gleaned from the use of essential oils and a healthier lifestyle.

Read through the relevant chapters again if you need confirmation or clarification of any of the information covered by the chapters. Often this helps you to develop your use of essential oils with more confidence, feeling that at least you have somewhere to refer to upon particular oils, their uses and how you can best tap into the aroma that will help you to feel the benefit that it has to offer.

If you enjoyed this book, please take the time to share it with your friends and post a positive review on Amazon. I would greatly appreciate it!

<u>CLICK HERE TO WRITE A POSITIVE REVIEW!</u>

www.ingramcontent.com/pod-product-compliance
Lightning Source LLC
Chambersburg PA
CBHW071157280526
45787CB00002B/532